Living Peace

Living Peace

A Spirituality of
Contemplation and Action

JOHN DEAR

IMAGE BOOKS
DOUBLEDAY
New York London Toronto Sydney Auckland

AN IMAGE BOOK
PUBLISHED BY DOUBLEDAY
a division of Random House, Inc.

IMAGE, DOUBLEDAY, and the portrayal of a deer drinking from a stream are
registered trademarks of Doubleday, a division of Random House, Inc.

Living Peace was originally published in hardcover by Doubleday, a division
of Random House, Inc., in 2001. This Image Books edition published by special
arrangement with Doubleday.

Book design by Claire Vaccaro

The Library of Congress has cataloged the Doubleday hardcover edition as follows:

Dear, John, 1959–
Living peace / John Dear.
p.   cm.
Includes bibliographical references.
1. Peace—Religious aspects—Catholic Church—Meditations.   2. Spiritual life—
Catholic Church—Meditations.   3. Christian life—Catholic authors.   4. Christian
life—Meditations.   I. Title.

BX1795.P43 D43 2001
261.8'73—dc21   00-048390

ISBN 0-385-49828-4

December 2004

First Image Books Edition

5   7   9   10   8   6   4

For Richard Deats and Jim Lawson

Friends and Peacemakers

I wish to thank Trace Murphy for suggesting this book and making it possible, and Lynn Fredriksson for editing the manuscript.

I wish to thank Trace Murphy for suggesting this book and making it possible, and Lynn Fredriksson for editing the manuscript.

Contents

❧

Contents

III. The Horizons of Peace

Introduction

Every morning, I take time to sit in the silence of the present moment, in the peace of God. I breathe in the spirit of peace. I return to the deep inner peace which is the heart of the spiritual life. I imagine sitting beside God. I listen for God's word of peace, that invitation to share in a life of love.

In that intimate, sacred peace, I rediscover myself. In that moment, I reclaim my identity as a child of God.

For the rest of my day, I try to live in a spirit of peace. Though I get caught up in my hectic routine, I return to that centered space whenever I can, and close the day in that same spirit. Over time, my life is slowly transformed.

The spirit of peace has led me from my childhood roots in North Carolina and Washington, D.C., to the Society of Jesus, the Jesuits, to become a Catholic priest, to soup kitchens, shelters, war zones, and jail cells around the country and the world, and to direct the Fellowship of Reconciliation (FOR), the largest, oldest interfaith peace organization in the United States.

Since 1915, FOR has promoted justice and disarmament throughout the world by advocating nonviolence as the only sure way to peace. FOR invites people of every religion, race, class, and culture to live the life, walk the road, and seek the God of peace. Its members range from students to grandmothers to Nobel Peace laureates to religious leaders—from Jane Addams, Dorothy Day, and Martin Luther King, Jr., to Thomas Merton, Thich Nhat Hanh, and Helen Prejean.

In my office, large photos of these great witnesses adorn the walls. Mahatma Gandhi, Dr. King, Dorothy Day, and Thomas Merton keep vigilant watch over me, urging me to persevere in the life of peace. They surround me like the communion of saints made visible.

Sitting in the present moment, breathing in the spirit of peace, looking at these messengers, I take up again the mission of peace and nonviolence in a world of war and violence. I feel ready to radiate the spirit of peace everywhere.

Perhaps more than anything, our world needs peace. We all need it, within our own broken hearts and broken families, in our bloody city streets and corrupt government offices, and in war zones and refugee camps.

On all sides, we are surrounded by violence; there are now over thirty-five wars being waged in the world. The slow violence of poverty and hunger kills over 40,000 people, mostly children, each day. Misery and destitution claim over two billion people throughout the developing world. Racism, sexism, discrimination, hate crimes, homelessness, unemployment, inadequate healthcare; the ongoing destruction of the environment; torture, executions, and other human rights abuses; in particular, the death of over one million Iraqis, mostly children under the age of five, from the United States/United Nations economic sanctions enforced since 1990; and on top of all of this, the ongoing threat of over 20,000 nuclear weapons in the world, mostly in the U.S., oppress us all with the threat of violence and death.

In such a world, my friends and I cling to a vision of nonviolence. In the spirit of interfaith prayer, we proclaim the possibility of a new world without war or violence, what Martin Luther King, Jr., called "the beloved community," or what Jesus called "the reign of God at hand."

But as the great pioneers knew, we must seek peace at every level of life, beginning within ourselves. Their example summons us to turn to God, allowing God to disarm our own hearts so that we can become instruments of God's disarming love in the world. They have called us to *become* the peace we seek.

If we simply live in the spirit of peace, we contribute to the peace of the entire world. This is an ancient spiritual truth. If we want to participate in this transformation, we have to begin right now, this very moment, to root out the violence within us, to forgive those who have hurt us, to let go of bitterness and resentment, to reconcile with one another, and open a way for the spirit of God to move freely among us. We need to take a deep breath, turn our hearts in prayer, and receive God's gift of peace that we can then share with all of humanity and creation itself.

Even as we enter that life, we are transformed; we discover a wholeness, a joy, a presence not of this world. If we pursue the depths of peace throughout our lives, we can change the world and become, like Gandhi, Dr. King, and Dorothy Day, witnesses to a better world.

Nothing could be more exciting, more challenging, or more meaningful than such a life.

And so, I offer these reflections and lessons from my own journey. They come in three parts: "Part I, The Depths of Peace: The Inner Journey", "Part II, The Heights of Peace: The Public Journey", and "Part III, The Horizons of Peace." I offer these meditations and stories from my own joys, struggles, and failings, to help others pursue the depths and heights and fullness of peace in their own lives.

May they help us all move closer toward that glorious day when we stand together face to face with the God of peace.

JOHN DEAR, S.J.
New York, New York

I.

The Depths of Peace:

The Inner Journey

Our true life lies at a great depth within us.
TAGORE

*Acquire inner peace and a multitude around you will
find their salvation.*
ST. SERAPHIN

*I believe that if one person gains spiritually, the whole world gains
with him or her, and if one person falls, the whole world
falls to that extent.*
MAHATMA GANDHI

*We can never obtain peace in the world if we neglect the inner world
and don't make peace with ourselves. World peace must develop
out of inner peace.*
THE DALAI LAMA

1.

Making Peace with Yourself

A few years before his death in 1999, the great Latin American advocate for the poor, Brazil's Archbishop Dom Helder Camara, was speaking at a crowded church in Berkeley, California. He was asked, "After facing death squads, would-be assassins, corporations oppressing the poor, violent government opposition, and even hostile forces within your own church, who is your most difficult opponent?"

Without saying a word, Dom Helder pointed his hand into the air, then slowly arched it around, until it turned on himself, his index finger pointing to his heart. "I am my own worst enemy," he said, "my most difficult adversary. Here I have the greatest struggle for peace."

Likewise, Mahatma Gandhi was once asked about his greatest enemy. He spoke of the British and his struggle against imperialism. Then he reflected on his own people, and his struggles against untouchability, bigotry, and violence in India. Finally, he spoke of himself, and his own inner violence, selfishness, and imperfection. The last, he confessed, was his greatest opponent. "There I have very little say."

If we want to make peace with others, we first need to be at peace with ourselves. But this can sometimes be as difficult as making peace in the bloodiest of the world's war zones.

Those who knew Dom Helder Camara and Mahatma Gandhi testify that they radiated a profound personal peace. But such peace came at a great price: a lifelong inner struggle. They knew that to practice peace and nonviolence, you have to look within.

Peace begins within each of us. It is a process of repeatedly showing mercy to ourselves, forgiving ourselves, befriending ourselves, accepting ourselves, and loving ourselves. As we learn to appreciate ourselves and accept God's gift of peace, we begin to radiate peace and love to others.

This lifelong journey toward inner peace requires regular self-examination and an ongoing process of making peace with ourselves. It means constantly examining the roots of violence within us, weeding out those roots, diffusing the violence that we aim at ourselves and others, and choosing to live in peace. It means treating ourselves with compassion and kindness. As we practice mercy toward ourselves, we begin to enjoy life more and more and celebrate it as adventure in peace. We turn again and again to the God who created us and offer sincere thanks. By persistently refraining from violence and hatred and opening up to that spirit of peace and mercy, we live life to the fullest, and help make the world better for others.

But this process of making peace with ourselves can be one of the most difficult challenges we face. Each one of us wrestles with our own demons. The daily challenge is to befriend those demons, embrace our true selves, make friends with ourselves, disarm our hearts, and accept in peace who we are. The deeper we go into our true identities, the more we will realize that each one of us is a unique yet beloved child of the God of peace. In that truth, we find the strength to live in peace.

For some, this inner struggle is just too difficult. Many prefer to endure their inner wars, believing that they cannot change, that inner peace is not realizable, that life is just too hard. Others succumb to violence and despair. I well remember my friend Mitch Snyder, the leading advocate for the homeless. For nearly twenty years, Mitch spoke out against poverty, organized demonstrations for housing, fasted for social change, and was arrested for civil disobedience on behalf of justice for the poor. He was director of the largest homeless shelter in the United States, a facility with over one thousand beds just three blocks from the U.S. Capitol in Washington, D.C. In the mid-1980s, while I was managing a small church shelter for the homeless in Washington, D.C., I often visited with Mitch and discussed the plight of the homeless and our campaign to secure decent, affordable housing for them.

Mitch gave his life for the forgotten and the poor, but became consumed by his anger against the system that oppresses the poor into homelessness. He advocated nonviolence, but suffered many personal demons which eventually got the best of him. For years, Mitch fought to gain local legislation guaranteeing the right of every person to shelter. Finally, in 1990, his effort was defeated. At the same time, a personal relationship broke down. On July 3, 1990, he gave in to despair, and killed himself. His suicide shocked and saddened us all.

Even though Mitch espoused justice and nonviolence eloquently on behalf of the most disenfranchised people in the nation, he could not maintain that same spirit of nonviolence toward himself, and the violence inside him literally destroyed him. His death challenged many of us who knew him to reexamine our own commitments and the violence within us, and to cultivate peace within, even as we continue to work actively for peace and justice.

"Love your neighbors as you love yourselves," Jesus tells us. As we love and accept ourselves, we will find strength to love others, and to love God, who loved us first. As we make peace with ourselves, we can learn to make peace with others. Such true self-love is not selfishness, egotism, or narcissism, but

wholeness, even holiness. First, we humbly accept our brokenness, our weakness, our limitations, our frailty and vulnerability, and our dependence on God. We accept our failures and
forgive ourselves for our mistakes. Then, we accept the living
God who dwells within us, and allow God's peace to make her
home within us. Making peace with ourselves is like building
an inner house of peace and welcoming the God of peace to
dwell there forever.

"While you are proclaiming peace with your lips," St. Francis of Assisi advised, "be careful to have it even more fully in
your heart." St. Francis put down his sword, took up the life of
peace, found his heart disarmed, and started serving the poor.
Everywhere he went, he proclaimed the good news of peace
and people would flock to hear him, just to be in his presence,
because he radiated peace.

But inner peace does not mean we float around in blissful
tranquillity, talking to the birds, untouched by everyday
mishaps, personal tragedies, or world events. In fact, true inner
peace pushes us into the thick of the world's problems, where
we rub elbows with all kinds of people and confront their
greatest terrors, as St. Francis did. From the hustle and bustle
of a crowded subway to the death of a loved one to turmoil at
the workplace to the threat of nuclear destruction, life presents
daily challenges to our inner resolve, but it is possible to cultivate and pursue inner peace no matter what obstacles come

our way. Through the grace of God, all our frustrations, turmoils, and tragedies can be transformed.

The inner life of peace means acting from a deep conviction about who we are, that each one of us is a beloved child of God, a human being called to love and serve other human beings. Living from this conviction does not mean we ignore our emotions—quite the contrary. In fact, as we go forward into the world, to places like death row, soup kitchens, or war zones, we touch the pain of the world and feel the full range of human emotions, with sorrow and anger, as we experience the pain of human tragedy and injustice. In 1985, while living in a refugee camp in El Salvador's war zone, I felt terrible sorrow, grief, and outrage as I witnessed the death and destruction around me, but I also felt a great inner peace because I clung to my faith in the God of peace, who seemed palpably present in the suffering people around me. Deep down, I rested in God's peace and even felt joy while I endured and resisted the horror of war with the refugees around me.

Our inner peace is not self-satisfied. We cannot idly pursue inner tranquillity while wars, bombings, executions, greed, and violence continue unchallenged. If we do not address the violence in the world, our inner peace is an empty illusion. Likewise, we cannot seek peace publicly and expect to help disarm the world while our hearts are filled with violence, judgment, and rage. Our work for peace cannot bear fruit if it is rooted in violence.

"One of the reasons why so many people have developed strong reservations about the peace movement is precisely that they do not see the peace they seek in the peacemakers themselves," the spiritual writer Henri Nouwen once observed. "Often what they see are fearful and angry people trying to convince others of the urgency of their protest. The tragedy is that peacemakers often reveal more of the demons they are fighting than of the peace they want to bring about."[1]

The roots of war, violence, injustice, and the threat of global annihilation lie within each one of us. Unless we recognize our complicity in global violence, we can never accept God's gift of peace. If, however, we recognize, acknowledge, and confess the violence within us, we allow God to begin the process of our disarmament, first in our own war-torn hearts, and then in the world itself.

As we pursue this inner journey and disarm our hearts, heal our internal divisions, seek inner reconciliation, and make peace with the God within, we can speak about disarmament, reconciliation, and peace with greater authenticity and integrity. Like Dom Helder Camara, Mahatma Gandhi, St. Francis, and Mother Teresa, we begin to embody our message. Because our message is rooted in our very being, in the God of peace who lives in us, our peace will spread out around us, even throughout the world, because it will be God's own peace springing forth.

Thomas Merton wrote that Gandhi's nonviolence "sprang from an inner realization of spiritual unity in himself. The whole Gandhian concept of nonviolent action and *satyagraha* ['truth-force'] is incomprehensible if it is thought to be a means of achieving unity rather than as the fruit of inner unity already achieved."[2] In other words, Gandhi had plumbed the depths of peace within himself. He renounced inner violence, advocated public nonviolence, and so, radiated peace to a world at war.

"Nonviolence is not a garment to be put on and off at will," Gandhi wrote. "Its seat is in the heart, and it must be an inseparable part of our very being. Nonviolence is a matter of the heart. It implies as complete self-purification as is humanly possible."[3]

Pursuing peace at every level of life—beginning within our own hearts and souls, and reaching out toward every human being alive on the planet—is the greatest and most fulfilling challenge one can undertake with one's life. But making peace in a world at war is an act greater than any of us. It is a spiritual journey that begins in the heart and takes us on a road not of our own choosing. But because it is a spiritual journey, a course charted by the God of peace, it is filled with the simplest but greatest of blessings.

As we make peace with ourselves, and welcome the God of peace who lives within us, we will learn to make peace with those around us and with others throughout the world. Over time, we will become true instruments of God's own peace and help make the world a better, more just place for all. The challenge is to do both: to pursue peace within and to pursue peace with the whole human race.

That journey, though difficult, promises a happy ending. We will be ready to meet the God of peace face to face when our time comes because we will have spent our lives welcoming God here and now in our hearts. We will look back and see that our lives have been a step-by-step pilgrimage from peace to peace until that great day when we enter God's own house of peace.

2.

Solitude

The life of peace begins anew each morning. We take a breath, awaken, and receive the gift of life, the gift of the present moment. The great spiritual traditions urge us to take time each day to center ourselves in the spirit of peace. If we dare enter the solitude of peace, we will rediscover who we are, each one of us a beloved, precious child of the God of peace.

"When you pray, go to your inner room, close your door, and pray to your God in secret," Jesus tells us in the Sermon on the Mount. "And your God who sees in secret will repay you" (Matthew 6:6). As we learn to sit in solitude and silence and turn down the noise of our mind, we create a sacred space for God to move within us. Paradoxically, if we seek out that lonely place within, as Jesus advises, we realize that we are not alone.

Solitude is often maligned in our culture. It is taken as a

sign of weakness, and confused with loneliness. Yet those who accept solitude as an opportunity for spiritual growth and inner healing experience it as a great blessing.

Why do we run from solitude? Why do we hate to be alone with ourselves? Because in solitude, our fears, insecurities, brokenness, hatred, and inner violence easily reveal themselves. Solitude can be terrifying at first. It reminds us of the deep loneliness we carry. But if we want real peace, we have to face our inner demons and transform our loneliness into love. Solitude is essential for this inner transformation.

The late spiritual writer Henri Nouwen exemplified this process. Throughout his career as a theologian at Yale and Harvard, and then during his pastoral ministry at L'Arche Daybreak, a community that serves the disabled in Toronto, Nouwen struggled with many personal ups and downs by taking quiet time alone each morning. Every few years he retreated for six months to a monastery. He recorded all these highs and lows in his many books and journals, explaining the value of prayerful solitude as the way through one's own inner anguish. By the time of his sudden death in 1996, he had weathered many personal battles, but reached a deeper level of self-understanding and peace.

As we sit by ourselves, feel those feelings, and embrace the spirit of peace, we take a deep breath and feel the peace of God enter our hearts. Slowly, over time, we even befriend our fears, anxieties, and inner turmoil as Henri Nouwen did. We make peace with our demons, they leave, and we gain inner freedom. In the process, we make friends with ourselves and learn to appreciate solitude as a precious gift.

History's spiritual leaders valued their solitude. Before Jesus began his public ministry, he spent forty days alone in the desert. Afterward, he regularly withdrew from the crowds to pray alone. In the Gospels, we frequently see Jesus finding deserted places to pray. Jesus' encounter with God in lonely hours of solitude allowed him to face the crowds with compassion, to speak truth with love, to seek justice come what may, and to resist evil nonviolently. He could speak of God because he experienced God in solitude.

Likewise, Gandhi knew that he could not call 350 million Indians to live in peace if he himself did not cultivate such peace. For fifty years, with great discipline, he took time to himself each day to pray alone. Each morning he rose at 3 A.M. for an hour of meditation. From this prayerful solitude, he summoned the strength to lead the crowds that looked to him for wisdom and guidance.

Thomas Merton spent his whole life exploring the depths of solitude. By rejecting the violence of the world completely and entering the Abbey of Gethsemani in 1941, he began a life of prayer and contemplation. Throughout the next twenty-seven years, until his tragic death in 1968, Merton delved

deeper and deeper within in pursuit of what he called "total inner transformation." As he withdrew into solitude, moving
from the monastery into a hermitage in the woods, ironically,
his private prayer pushed him to share his wisdom of peace
with the world. At the height of the nuclear arms race, the civil
rights struggle, and the Vietnam War, this solitary monk became a public prophet of peace.

"It is in deep solitude that I find the gentleness with which
I can truly love my brothers and sisters," Merton wrote. "The
more solitary I am, the more affection I have for them. It is
pure affection and filled with reverence for the solitude of others. Solitude and silence teach me to love my brothers and sisters for what they are, not for what they say."[4] Merton saw his
life of solitude as the greatest gift he could offer the world. As
the violence of the 1960s exploded and peace movement
friends begged him to take public action, Merton retreated farther into solitude, exploring Eastern meditation, plunging the
depths of peace in his own heart.

"The contemplative has nothing to tell you except to reas-
sure you and say that if you dare to penetrate your own silence
and dare to advance without fear into the solitude of your own
heart, and risk the sharing of that solitude with the lonely other
who seeks God through you and with you," Merton wrote,
"then you will truly recover the light and the capacity to understand what is beyond words and beyond explanations because

it is too close to be explained: it is the intimate union in the depths of your own heart, of God's spirit and your own secret inmost self, so that you and God are in all truth One Spirit."[5]

In solitude, Merton discovered, we remember that we are weak, dependent on our Creator. Solitude exposes our powerlessness. In solitude, we cannot use God for egotistical purposes, to promote a "holier than thou" self-image. We cannot maintain our sense of power or accomplishment or control. Solitude humbles us, reveals our poverty of spirit, and returns us to our true humanity before God. It cuts through our illusions to reveal the bare bones of reality. If we have the courage to stay with ourselves in solitude, we will discover our own authenticity and integrity. We receive the grace to accept the truth of our humanity.

Throughout my life, I have tried to take quiet time each day in solitude for prayer. For the last eighteen years, I have made an annual eight-day, silent retreat where I seek the God of peace. I have often spent summers alone to experiment with peace in solitude.

Each day, as I face myself alone, I remember that my personal peacemaking is the hardest work of all. I recognize anew the violence within my own war-torn heart, and try again to make peace with myself and my God.

The week after I entered the Jesuit Novitiate, in 1982, my spiritual director sent me to sit in the chapel for an hour to ponder the verse "Be still and know that I am God." *One hour?*, I thought to myself. *Who can do that?* My mind raced unceasingly while I shifted from one position to the next, bored and frustrated. Not only did I find no peace within myself, I couldn't even sit still. With time, however, my restlessness eased. In a matter of weeks, I began to pray in solitude and learned to find there a way to peace.

A few months later, I made my first thirty-day silent retreat of St. Ignatius of Loyola, "The Spiritual Exercises." During those days, I spoke with no one (except briefly each morning with my spiritual director). I did not read newspapers, watch television, listen to the radio, or receive mail. Instead, I meditated on the Gospels for hours, day and night, alone in complete silence.

Within a few days, an entirely new rhythm opened up to me. A completely different spirit overtook me. It was like walking in slow motion. Everything became quiet and peaceful. I settled into a deep peace within myself and toward others. I never knew such peace was possible.

During the intensity of those days, I looked at the world through new eyes and saw more clearly its terrible injustice and horrific brutality but also its ongoing transformation by our peacemaking God. That dramatic solitude pushed me deeper into the life of peace and the public struggle for justice than ever before. It taught me the power of prayer. I realized what Gandhi meant when he said, "Mute prayer is my greatest weapon." When we give the God of peace our complete attention, we are changed, and so, therefore, is the world.

Wherever I am, in the privacy of my room, in a monastery, church, school, or park, I try each day to sit in solitude to open to the inner life of peace. In this sacred space, God teaches me how to reach out with love to others. I don't know how this happens, but I know that it does. I know, too, that I cannot live without it. Solitude has become an essential ingredient in my own journey to peace.

When I fail to embrace the solitude of God's peace, I get caught up in the world's downward spiral of violence and turmoil. I soon feel disconnected and scattered. I lose my sense of inner peace, and then all hope. If I try to rely on myself alone, I quickly fall. The horrors of the world fill me with despair. The violence around me inflames the violence within me and I turn against myself and those around me. The absence of solitude and peaceful meditation leads me to doubt, desolation, self-pity, self-hatred, and a sense of meaninglessness. Before I know it, I've convinced myself that there is no hope, I cannot love unconditionally, peace is a dream, God doesn't exist, and my work for justice is a futile waste of time. I can lose patience with myself and others, give in to anger and resentment, and find life a terrible burden.

The grace of solitude changes all that. In that quiet, centered space, I am transformed. Though solitude forces me to confront myself, it also takes me outside of myself and opens my heart to grace. Everything is charged with beauty as I return to God's peaceful presence. Faith, hope, and love come alive once more. I rise above myself and the world and feel God's peace. Because I am experiencing a peace that is not of this world, I am strengthened to reach out, to make peace, and to love others, even my enemies.

Solitude plucks us out of the world's frenzy and centers us in nonviolence. Solitude silences the loud voices within us to allow the still, small voice of God to speak. Solitude gives God the time and space to disarm our inner wars. Solitude introduces us to the God of peace. Solitude gives us the strength to receive God's gift of peace, and to learn to be at peace with ourselves and those around us.

The great paradox of solitude, as Thomas Merton taught so well, is that as we enter alone into the sacred presence of God, we find ourselves moving closer to others, indeed to the whole human race. Solitude leads us into a greater solidarity with humanity because it reveals our own humanity and our common God. In that peaceful transformation, we feel new strength to touch the solitude of others with a deep, compassionate love. Indeed, the peace of our solitude leads us to the deep peace that undergirds the solitude of the entire human family.

3.

Silence

Solitude is a welcoming space for the God of peace. It opens up sacred space within us. As we seek the presence of God, we need to keep silent. Silence helps us to be attentive to the quiet presence of God. Silence can be God's language, the language of peace.

Our own silence leads us to the silence of God. Silence disposes us to hear what we need to hear, what God wants to say to us. We turn off the noise around and within us. As we dwell in solitude and cultivate interior silence, we learn to listen for the consoling whispers of God.

In solitude or even in a crowded park or quiet gathering of people, silence can be a doorway to the peace of God.

"Be still and know that I am God," we read in the Psalms. A life of prayer calls for the simple discipline of sitting in silence, attuned to the reality of God's presence. Yet this simple task seems extremely difficult. We fill our lives with noise, from television to radio to stereo and compact disc. Our culture says noise is necessary. We prefer noise because it dulls our innate loneliness. We are uncomfortable with silence. Yet only by cultivating silence daily do we begin to accept its many gifts.

We need silence to express our true selves. Silence is countercultural and more; it leads us beyond culture, beyond illusion, beyond words, to the truth of peace. In silence, we can no longer deny our basic humanity, our powerlessness, our helplessness. Silence unveils our vulnerable selves. As the distractions of the culture and our own mind leave us, we feel an approaching peace. Silence opens the door to peace, and to God. If we want to seek first God's reign, as Jesus instructs in the Sermon on the Mount, we need to enter the world of silence. We move from communication to communion. In silence, we discover the heart of reality.

In the Book of Kings, the prophet Elijah walked forty days and forty nights to the mountain of Horeb in search of God. A heavy wind blew against the mountain, but God was not in the wind. Then, an earthquake shook the mountain, but God was not in the earthquake. Next, a fire burned the mountain, but God was not in the fire. Finally, there was a tiny, whispering sound. "When he heard this," we are told, "Elijah hid his face in his cloak and went and stood at the entrance of the cave. A

voice said to him, 'Elijah, why are you here?' He replied, 'I
have been most zealous for Yahweh, the God of hosts. But the
Israelites have forsaken your covenant, torn down your altars,
and put your prophets to the sword. I alone am left, and they
seek to take my life.' 'Go, take the road back to the desert,' "
God said to Elijah (1 Kings 19:9–15).

Elijah, like all saints, mystics, and peacemakers, learned
that God comes to us in a still, small voice, only audible in silence. As we struggle for justice and peace like Elijah, we, too,
hear the voice of God whisper to us and guide us in the right
direction. To hear the whispering voice of the peacemaking
God, we need to dwell in solitude and silence. Then we will
find courage to face the war-making world.

In the fourth and fifth centuries, after Christianity was co-
opted by the Roman Empire, many Christians fled to the
desert to practice the life of contemplative nonviolence. There
in the silence of their new solitude they rediscovered the heart
of the spiritual life, the essence of prayer. Like our desert fathers and mothers, we, too, need to find our own desert places
to meet the God of peace in solitude and silence.

Perhaps more than anyone, Mahatma Gandhi understood
the critical importance of silence. After decades of public
speaking, continuous meetings, and active resistance to evil, he
began his own personal day of silence. Every Monday, he wrote
letters, outlined articles, walked, prayed, and rested, but spoke

to no one. Even if thousands of people were waiting for his wisdom, or the British viceroy himself wanted to negotiate India's independence, he remained silent. This weekly grounding in silence helped him build the foundation he needed to resist the world's turmoil.

Thomas Merton advocated silence for Westerners trapped in a materialistic, noisy culture. "When I am liberated by silence," Merton wrote, "when I am no longer involved in the measurement of life, but in the living of it, I can discover a form of prayer in which there is effectively, no distraction. My whole life becomes a prayer. My whole silence is full of prayer. The world of silence in which I am immersed contributes to my prayer."⁶ "Silence is the strength of our interior life."⁷

To be people of peace, Merton suggests, we need to cultivate silence. In silence, we hear the voice of God. We receive not only the gift of inner peace but a call to active engagement, a mission of peace.

As an act of prayer and an act of peace, I recommend that each day we step into silence. That means concretely that we shut the door to our rooms, turn off the TV and the radio and the noise around us, and feel this new quiet. In this silent solitude, we can begin to settle down and quiet the interior sounds and voices that race through our mind. As we slow down interiorly, and become quiet like our surroundings, we enter a healing peace. We close our eyes, concentrate on our gentle breathing, dwell in the spirit of peace, imagine ourselves set in the fullness of peace, and begin to incarnate that vision.

Then the excitement begins! As we enter into this holy silence, we set the stage to hear the One who speaks to our hearts. What do we hear? If we listen carefully in the silence of our heart, we will hear the words of peace. It may take a while. We may have to take short segments throughout our days when we return to silence and solitude. Indeed, we may end up spending whole days in silence and learning to walk with an interior silence that makes us more present to others and to all of creation.

But if we practice prayerful, peaceful silence, the God of peaceful silence will come to us and speak. The question is: Are we willing to listen?

4.

Listening

Solitude and silence create a sacred space for God to speak to our hearts. But if we want to hear what God is saying to us, we have to listen attentively. Prayer is not so much *talking to* God as *listening for* God. Once we've settled into a peaceful place of prayer, we remain alert, wait for God, listen for God, and welcome God's word of peace.

But attentive listening is difficult. We much prefer to talk, usually about ourselves. We ramble on with friends and when we've finished, we go on our way thinking we had a good conversation, even when they haven't spoken a word. This same rambling monologue can take over our search for God. While we beg God to help us and to hear our troubles, we can move beyond talking at God to experiencing God's disarming presence, even hearing God's message of peace for us.

As in all intimate, loving relationships, each shares a love and respect for the other. While one person speaks, the other listens lovingly. Then, at some point, the speaker becomes silent and listens attentively as the other person speaks. Otherwise, the relationship remains one-sided. It will never grow and deepen. In fact, it will die. If we do not listen to one another in a spirit of great compassion, love, and interest, we will not remain real friends for long. Honest dialogue and compassionate listening are key ingredients to lasting peace and reconciliation.

The same can be said of prayer. If we want to have an intimate, loving relationship with God, we will have to give God our undivided attention and love. If we do not take time to listen to God, how will we ever know what God is trying to say to us? How can we claim that God is aloof, uninvolved, uncaring? We cannot expect to hear God's message of peace if we do not step back from the noise around us and seriously listen. We can never expect to know God or receive God's gift of peace.

Why do we not sit and listen for the voice of God more often? Perhaps because we fear what we might hear. We are terrified that God might discover just how wretched we are and tell us so. We tremble at the possibility that we might hear the voice of God speak to us in the same hate-filled language we use. We fear the loss of control. We tremble at the vulnerability that prayer exposes.

But perhaps most of all we fear that we will hear God

tell us that God loves us intimately. We can't handle such love or its responsibility. We reject the possibility that the Creator of the fifteen-billion-year-old universe could delight in each one of us like a doting parent, crazy over her child. We have internalized the values of our culture and filled ourselves with such anger and bitterness that we reject God's challenging love.

"My life is a listening, God's is a speaking," Thomas Merton wrote in *Thoughts in Solitude.*[8] Listening means baring our souls to the presence of God. It means letting God speak to us as God wants, not as we want. Listening for God means surrendering our deepest, most vulnerable selves to the unknown. It means opening ourselves to new discoveries, new experiences, new adventures. Fundamentally, it means getting ready to encounter God, not just at the moment of our death but right this very moment! Such a step, though simple, is not just countercultural; it's revolutionary.

The Gospels portray Jesus as a great listener. First and foremost, he was a person of contemplative prayer who spent time listening for the voice of God. Only a few verses into Mark's Gospel, God says, "You are my beloved son; upon you my favor rests." Later, at his transfiguration, Jesus hears God call him "beloved" again. Jesus heard this beautiful affirmation because he was listening attentively for God's voice. He could not have heard these words if he had not listened.

Jesus wants his disciples to listen, too. But they refuse to listen to him or to God. He marvels at the crowds, those who have "ears but do not hear, as well as eyes but do not see." At the transfiguration, God speaks plainly to the disciples: "This is my Beloved. Listen to him!" But throughout the Gospels, the disciples, the religious authorities, and the crowds refuse to listen. Because of this inability to listen, they are filled with confusion and despair. Only after the resurrection of Jesus, when they sit together in silent prayer, listening for the spirit of Jesus, do they become contemplatives. In that new attentive listening, they hear the risen Jesus offer his first gift: "Peace be with you."

Pentecost is first of all an experience of prayerful, communal listening. Pentecost teaches the disciples to listen for the spirit of God moving in their lives. Only after listening do they know what to teach. They trusted God and God's spirit moving through their community. They were ready for anything. They radiated a joy that captivated crowds, infuriated the authorities, and inspired generations. They believed that they were loved and forgiven, and were so transformed that they risked their lives to share that good news. In the end, they helped bring down an empire and changed the world.

If we want to live in peace, we need to spend time each day listening to God. As contemplative peacemakers, we let the God of peace lead us. As we open up and wait patiently for

God to speak to us, we begin to know God and God's will for us. And we become powerful in our powerlessness.

For many years, I prided myself on what I thought was a rich life of prayer. But as I look back on those years, I am appalled and ashamed. I spent years telling God all the problems of the world and what should be done about them. I railed against God. I yelled and commanded. I demanded action—on my terms, according to my timetable. I wanted God to do my will, to follow my lead, to get in line with my vision.

I marvel now at my arrogance. I was in charge in prayer. After I gave my orders, I left feeling confident that I had had a real prayer experience, that I lived a deep spiritual life. But as time went on, I grew angry at God because God was not living up to my (false) image. God was not being the God I had demanded.

Now I realize that I rarely allowed God's face to be revealed to me, or more importantly, God to get a word in edgewise. Because I so dominated this "prayer time," I rarely let the intimate love of God touch my heart. As a result, I could not deepen my conscious awareness of my relationship with God. My spirit continued to turn in constant chaos. I was far from inner peace.

Perhaps I was afraid of what God might say to me if I gave God half a chance. With the help of a gifted spiritual director, I began to recognize my patterns. Slowly I realized that, as in any intimate relationship, both parties want simply to be in each other's loving presence. Years of yelling at God revealed how little I loved God or wanted to receive God's gift of peace. So I began to listen for God, and look for God's presence in my life. I waited for God's spirit to touch me.

Over time, a new journey emerged. I was no longer in control. Prayer became a silent listening for "the still, small voice of God." God was in charge of our relationship, and spoke when God wanted to speak. I waited. God initiated the conversation. Over time, as I developed attentive listening and contemplative adoration, God became personal. I encountered not just the peace of God but the living God of peace.

For some of us, the development of prayer can be summed up as follows: years and years talking at God, years talking to God, then slowly, turning and listening to God. We listen for God. Finally, we are silent, being nurtured in the abiding, peaceful presence of God.

God calls each one of us God's own beloved daughter or son. As we listen, we hear: "Do not be afraid. I am with you. I love you." Listening for God, then, is a way of opening ourselves to God. It prepares us for God in the depths of our souls. As we listen to God and hear God's word of peace, we find strength to take another step on the journey of peace.

If we want to pursue that journey to peace, we need to take a few minutes each day, beginning right this very moment, entering into the silent presence of God and listening for God's gentle, loving voice.

Close your eyes, relax, notice your breathing, center yourself, quiet your mind, feel the silence around you, let it come within you, and start listening attentively. Maybe you hear the birds outside or the breeze in the trees. Maybe you hear the rain falling on the roof. Maybe you hear your own breath. But as you listen attentively and spend quality time listening deeply, you will over time hear God speak personally to your heart. You will hear the words of peace. You will hear God say to you, as God said to Jesus, "You are my beloved." The scriptures and the saints guarantee it. God wants to speak to us. God wants to tell us good things. All we have to do is listen. And if we do, we will be filled with peace.

5.

Letting Go

How would you feel if you woke up tomorrow morning and had lost all of your possessions? How would you respond if you had to let go of everything?

Over the years, I have met scores of people who have suffered such tragedies—refugees who lost their homes and families in war; homeless people who lost their jobs and their houses overnight; prisoners who were wealthy businessmen one day and convicted, penniless felons the next; and victims of wildfires whose homes burned to the ground in a minute. These ordinary folks were just like you and me until tragedy struck.

Such tragedies can befall any of us at any moment. In fact, one day, each of us will lose control of everything we possess. We will die. The question is: How can we live our lives in peace and die in peace with ourselves and with everyone?

We can prepare for that great day by starting today the process of letting go. If we dare let go of our possessions and the will to control and dominate, we will cultivate a deeper spirit of peace within us because we will not have anything left to cling to. Buddhist monk Thich Nhat Hanh lost hundreds of fellow monks and friends during the Vietnam War and was forced into exile in the mid-1960s. He has not been allowed to return home to Vietnam since then. Yet throughout his painful ordeal, he has maintained a spirit of true detachment, and modeled the life of true peace. He radiates peace because he has let go of everything and accepted the present moment as a gift of peace. He has entered the house of peace. Though he lives in France, not Vietnam, he has found a rare freedom.

To settle in to the house of peace, we need to let go of the baggage we carry with us. The God of peace welcomes us at the door, embraces us and invites us inside where we unpack and start a whole new life. Just as solitude, silence, and listening lay the groundwork for the prayer of peace, so letting go of what we cling to enables us to enter God's house and embrace the God of peace.

Our First World culture socializes us to cling to our possessions. Through fear, insecurity, and faithlessness, we accumulate a wide variety of paraphernalia. We carry on our shoulders a lifetime supply of material goods, as well as anger, jealousy, bitterness, and violence. These weights prevent us

from coming before God as we truly are—vulnerable, ordinary
human beings. They prevent us from diving deep into our own
spiritual wells.

As we sit in silence and listen for the voice of God, the first
voices we hear are the recordings that play repeatedly within
us, goading us to fear, to loathe ourselves, to hold grudges, to
practice violence, to reject God. The journey into silence and
listening requires that we quiet these negative voices. As we
delve deeper into our own silence, we befriend ourselves, quiet
those voices, offer them to God, and wait humbly to receive
God's gift of peace with open arms.

Prayer demands vulnerability. Real prayer takes us to that
gut-level intimacy between ourselves and our God. Jesus continually manifested his human vulnerability. Because he let go
of power and embraced his weakness, he accepted his dependence on God. He saw God as a caring father and himself as an
obedient son. Likewise, we, too, come before our God in our
vulnerability and weakness. As we let go of our false defenses,
illusions, and power, we experience God as a loving parent, an
abiding Spirit, the faithful brother Jesus. But to reach that intimate relationship, we must expose our hearts and our souls.

Our culture discourages vulnerability. Even the word "vulnerability" bespeaks susceptibility to injury, criticism, or attack.
Vulnerability risks suffering. We are rarely vulnerable with one
another, and certainly not before entire peoples. We fear get-

ting hurt. Likewise, we do not find it easy to be vulnerable before God. We fear attack, rejection, or death by the "omnipotent" God. Because we build shields to protect our vulnerable souls, we miss encountering a vulnerable God who longs to meet us as we are—simple, powerless, human.

Jesus spent his life releasing his personal desires to become truly vulnerable before God and humanity. His vulnerability shines throughout the Gospels. In one touching scene, he encounters a Samaritan woman beside a well. As she responds with openness and honesty, he recognizes in her a trustworthy soul and bares his own. He reveals his true identity as the Christ to her. Never before had he revealed himself so intimately to another human being. He is moved by the vulnerability of this genuine woman who once had seven husbands, and who was not only a Gentile but a Samaritan, a hated enemy of the Jews. Jesus leads her to transforming faith. She runs off to tell her townspeople about him. They, too, are disarmed, and head out to meet Jesus. They invite him to stay with them, and come to believe in Jesus. In the end, her whole community is transformed.

Jesus' vulnerability climaxes with his arrest in the garden (where he is kissed by his betrayer). He is then condemned, jailed, tortured, and crucified. Hanging naked on a cross, covered in blood, mocked by passersby, Jesus dies calling out to God with the words of Psalm 22. "My God, my God, why have you forsaken me?" Here we see how vulnerable Jesus is before God. The Psalm the Gospels quote moves from despair to hope, concluding with a promise of victory for the faithful one. Jesus has let go of everything and clings only to God. "From my mother's womb, you are my God," the Psalm continues. "I will proclaim your name to my brothers and sisters. I will utter praise in the vast assembly. I will fulfill my vows before those who fear God. My soul shall live."

Jesus manifests utter dependence on God. He has let go of his very life. He focuses completely on God. There is nothing left but God. In this perfect letting go, within his heart and now in his death, he not only finds peace, he incarnates it.

As he hangs on the cross and draws his last breath, Jesus hands over his soul to God: "Into your hands I commend my spirit," he prays. This ultimate letting go epitomizes the lifelong journey of peace. He dies forgiving his murderers, consoling his mother, and clinging faithfully to God. Like Jesus, we, too, can let go of ourselves, cling to God, and plumb the depths of peace. In the end, like Jesus, we can finally let go of everything and offer our spirits to the God of peace.

Quiet daily prayer begins the process of letting go. As we enter into the quiet prayer of vulnerability and letting go, we find ourselves more and more given over to peace. After a lifetime of discipline and letting go, death becomes a final turning of the page, one last release in a lifelong series, gentle and peaceful. It begins the culmination of a life of peace.

Henri Nouwen called prayer "letting go of all things." "In the act of prayer," he wrote, "we undermine the illusion of control by divesting ourselves of all false belongings and by directing ourselves totally to the God who is the only one to whom we belong. Prayer therefore is the act of dying to all that we consider to be our own and of being born to a new existence which is not of this world. Prayer is indeed a death to the world so that we can live for God." Prayer is "the most radical and most revolutionary act, the act by which everything is turned around and made new, the act by which the barriers of fear are broken down, the act by which we can enter into a world which is not of this world—the act, therefore, that is the basis for all other actions."

"In a situation in which the world is threatened by annihilation," Nouwen concludes, "prayer does not mean much when we undertake it only as an attempt to influence God, or as a search for a spiritual fallout shelter, or as an offering of comfort in stress-filled times. Prayer in the face of a nuclear holocaust only makes sense when it is an act of stripping ourselves of everything, yes, even of life itself. Prayer is the act by which we divest ourselves of all false belongings and become free to belong to God and God alone."[9]

Living Peace

Henri Nouwen's unexpected death on September 21, 1996, illustrates the meaning of his words. He spent his life struggling with prayer and the daily disciplines of meditation, scripture reading, and eucharist. He gave up his prestigious academic career at Yale and Harvard to live with and serve the disabled in Toronto's L'Arche Daybreak community. Days after suffering a massive heart attack in a hotel in Holland, he continued to pray and trust in God, offering words of gratitude, asking for forgiveness. His last words to family and friends were, "My God in whom I trust!" When he died suddenly from a second massive heart attack, he was as ready as he could be. His life continues to bear fruit, to teach a spirituality of peace.

The life of peace is a journey of letting go. As we let go more and more each day, all that remains will be God and God's spirit of love. As we move along on our life's journey, letting go of our possessions and receiving gifts of peace, we become freer to enter God's reign of peace. We are liberated and transformed into the peaceful human beings we were created to be, until that great day when we will fully enter God's house of peace.

6.

Imagining God

The culture of violence would have us believe that just as we are violent, God must also be violent. It portrays God as vengeful, waiting to throw us into the eternal fires of hell. Such a god must surely justify and bless our wars. Instead of God the peacemaker, we have been taught to believe in god the warmaker. Since we were children, we have been presented with these false images of God. This fearful figure still lingers in the back of our minds.

Because of this, many reject God. Who would want anything to do with such a terrifying prospect of "divine violence"?

The Bible is filled with images of a violent god. From the wrathful god who orders the rains to flood the earth and kill everyone except those in Noah's Ark, to the war-making god who smites Pharaoh's armies, to the god of the Psalms who hears our prayer to crush the skulls of our enemies' babies, we read not about the God of nonviolent love but the god of violent retribution.

I think the Hebrew scriptures show the Jewish people struggling with their new faith in God against the culture's faith in the false gods of empire. As the stories and books progress through the centuries, a more radical image of God emerges. Beginning with the prophets, we hear of God as the God of poor, the God who loves justice, the God who leads us to beat swords into plowshares. With the breakthrough of Christ in the Christian scriptures, we are presented with the image of God as a loving father, as the God who sends sunshine and rain on both the just and the unjust, and in Christ, as a nonviolent activist who heals the sick, resists injustice, and refuses to retaliate. As a Christian, I believe that Jesus reveals finally the true face of God as the God of nonviolence, love, and peace. In Jesus, we realize that God does not hurt us or ever wish us harm.

Over the past few decades as I have tried to engage in the struggle for peace and justice, I have sought out the roots of our spiritual problems, including the world's wars and injustice. Over time, I have concluded that our spiritual problems as a people result from our basic misunderstanding of the nature of God. Because we live in a culture addicted to violence that blesses wars and makes weapons of mass destruction, we have grown accustomed to violence, killing, and death. This getting used to violence has infected our spirituality, and even become the center of our spirituality. Without consciously doing so, we have accepted the culture's presupposition that the Creator of the universe must be violent, as the Hebrew scriptures describe, since the world is so brutal.

But the revelation of Christ is that the living God is very different from us and very different from the world. According to the Gospels, God loves us unconditionally, suffers for us, longs to give us peace, wants each of us to live, and showers us with compassion. According to Jesus, God is a God of love and peace who forgives us and desires that we all live in love and peace with one another.

If this Christian revelation of God is true—and I believe it with all my heart—then we need to reexamine our image of God in the context of our culture's violence. We need to notice how the culture distorts the God of peace, leads us to distrust God, and creates an image of God who wants our enemies dead and maybe us as well. Then we as a people need to turn back to the living God of peace and start walking God's path of peace.

The question is: What is our image of God? Is the God we worship angry, violent, scheming to throw us in to hellfire? Is our God, in other words, the god of war? Does our God bless

the suffering around us, want the poor to starve or the homeless to freeze? Does our God support dictators, allow genocide,
permit nuclear weapons, or side with armies?

Or is our God completely opposed to all violence, and so
different from ourselves that we cannot understand what God
is like? Has the living God been the victim of bad press? Isn't
God a God of nonviolence, compassion, reconciliation, and
boundless mercy? Doesn't it make sense that our God would
be humble, gentle, and generous? Because we have known
nothing but war, isn't it possible that we have blinded ourselves to the peace of God, indeed, the God of peace?

If people of faith around the world reflect deeply on their
image of God, I believe they would renounce violence, embrace nonviolence, and resist war. That sounds like a simplistic,
naive, sweeping statement, but after traveling around the
world and meeting all kinds of suffering, struggling people, I
firmly believe it. I think this is one of the fundamental mes-
sages of the entire Christian scriptures. If we start to worship
the living God of nonviolence at the center of our beings, our
hearts will be disarmed, we will reject violence, and we will become a people of nonviolence. If we worship the God of peace,
we will reject war and become people of peace. If we reject the

false gods who practice revenge and retaliation, we will become people of forgiveness, compassion, and reconciliation.

We cannot worship the living God of peace and nonviolence and at the same time support war and violence. It's as simple as that. The choice comes down to following the living God and God's nonviolence or the false gods and the world's violence.

The problem is that we do not worship the living God of peace and nonviolence. Deep down, each of us worships the false god of war and violence, the idols of money and weapons, the golden calves created by our culture. We prefer these false gods because they have given us a (false) sense of security. We have grown comfortable with our illusions. We have been so seduced by our own culture, we cannot even imagine a culture of nonviolence, much less the God of nonviolence. Indeed, our culture has robbed us of our imagination.

Contemplative prayer invites us not only to let go of our possessions and violence but also our false images of God. The practice of quiet, intimate, peaceful prayer allows the living God to reveal God's self to us as God is. When we accept our poverty of spirit, we open ourselves to God as God is, not as we have made God to be. As we sit in peace, we can put aside the world's false images of God. Instead, we can imagine what our God is like—gracious, gentle, and generous. We can experience the kindness of God as we meditate.

This living God touches our hearts, disarms us, and fills us with a peace not of this world. Suddenly old images fall away. Our God stands before us unarmed, welcoming, and compassionate. We realize that God is peace itself. Then we begin to understand what Thomas Merton meant when he described God at the end of his journal, *The Sign of Jonas*, as "Mercy within Mercy within Mercy."

How do we imagine the God of peace?

In the sixteenth century, Ignatius of Loyola suggested that we use our imaginations to deepen our relationship with God. Following Ignatius' method, we picture in our minds God as a loving father, a caring mother, as Jesus our brother, or the Holy Spirit as the abiding presence of peace. Each day, we sit in silent contemplation with this warm and gracious image of God.

As we contemplate our God, over time we are touched at some deep emotional and spiritual level by God's own disarming spirit. We are drawn ever deeper into God. Our lives are transformed.

Ignatian spirituality teaches that if we imagine being with Jesus as he is described in the Gospels, we can enter into his presence, be healed by his peace, and be sent out as instruments of peace in the world. Ignatius urges daily meditation on the life of Jesus to know God and God's will.

The Ignatian method is simple: Read a text from the Gospel; then center yourself in a quiet space and imagine the scene from the text. Enter the scene as a character in the story or as yourself. Notice how Jesus reacts to you. Listen to what Jesus says to you. Let the Spirit lead you into the life of Jesus. See how Jesus feels. Learn how he lives. This method of prayer can be applied to any scene from the life of Jesus, from the infancy narratives to the call of the disciples to the healing miracles to the last supper, the crucifixion, and the resurrection.

Over time, we learn to spend weeks or months with one Gospel scene, as a way to enter into the presence of God. For example, we could imagine ourselves standing with the women at the foot of the cross, looking at Jesus, listening to his last words, trying to be present to him as he dies, making the connection there with the crucified peoples of the world. This meditation draws us closer to Christ crucified and sensitizes us to the suffering of others. As we enter into the helplessness of the scene and experience Christ's faithful love, our own hearts break, the spirit of Christ heals us, and we begin to spend our own lives healing the broken and marginalized. We can stand before the risen Christ and answer his call to make disciples of all nations.

In this type of contemplative prayer, we experience the nature, even the personality, of Jesus, and thus the nature of God. These images reveal to us the gentleness and nonviolence of God in Christ. From our own simple, daily spiritual experience, we know now that the living God is a God of peace and nonviolence. Such knowledge and prayer will have consequences and implications for our lives. We will over time become like the God we worship. We will try to become as gentle, peaceful, nonviolent, and loving as the Jesus we experience in our prayer.

At its core, the spiritual life is a dynamic, daily encounter with God. It is an inner journey of peace, compassion, and nonviolence. In this contemplative journey, we come to know God as God is. The false gods and false images of a god that we have created disappear. We discover that the God we experience in our hearts each day is not violent, vengeful, or warlike. Instead, we experience God as unconditional love, unending mercy, active nonviolence, and perfect peace.

As we encounter the living God of peace, we understand how Trappist and Buddhist monks can spend their entire lives in contemplative prayer. Like them, we have been touched by God's peace and forever transformed. We want to spend our days drawing ever closer to our beloved God.

In whatever way we seek God in our lives, we will be changed because we know that our God is precisely a God of peace and nonviolent love. Once we have encountered this nonviolent, loving God, we can never return to our violent ways.

For some, this is heresy. They cannot let go of their violent, vengeful images of God. I think real faith in the God of peace and nonviolence is a kind of cultural heresy; it is an act of resistance against a culture that legalizes war, injustice, and nuclear weapons. That's why I believe our image of God is critically important not only for our own souls but politically and socially for the whole world. This question can lead us to the heart of Christianity, what it means to be a human being, and what a more peaceful world would look like.

The question before us is: *Who is your God, and what does your God look like?*

If you believe in a god who could condone one act of violence, just one act of murder, then you will slide down the slippery slope of justified, divine violence and in the end support the nuclear extinction of the human race. If you believe, as I do, that God is essentially nonviolent, and that this nonviolent love is what makes God God, then you can never support violence in any form, and the more you pursue this God of nonviolence, the more you will offer your life loving, serving, and dying for others as Jesus did, knowing that God intended us to love one another and be nonviolent toward one another, and that sooner or later, we will all be forgiven, disarmed, and welcomed into God's peaceful presence, God's reign of nonviolence.

The possibility that the living God of the universe is perfectly nonviolent, totally forgiving, unconditionally loving, and infinitely compassionate toward each one of us individually and all ninety billion people who ever lived collectively, for most people, is too good to be true. In fact, we do not want God to be nonviolent, forgiving, loving, or compassionate. We are uncomfortable with and scared by such a prospect because it is so unknown to us. This breathtaking new image of God shatters our world and would turn us all upside down if we dared to accept it as true. But Jesus gave his life insisting that in fact this wonderful, radical, beautiful image of a loving God is in fact true. Others from St. Francis to Oscar Romero have accepted it and done the same.

Dare we accept such an image of God? I think that the Christian scriptures and the saints can be trusted when they insist that we have no reason to be afraid. We can let go of our false images of God and let God's kindness touch us. We can let God be as God is and trust that God knows what God is doing. If God is nonviolent, and created humanity to be nonviolent, and wants each one of us to be nonviolent, why do we keep rejecting God's nonviolence and insist that we know better, that our ways of violence and revenge are justified? Why not let go of our old ways of violence and the false gods we have created to justify the world's violence and accept the nonviolence of God?

These are great questions. I think they stand at the center of the spiritual life. Do we prefer divine nonviolence or worldly violence? If we step into the question and begin the journey of Godly nonviolence and practice the peace we see God modeling, I believe, as Rainer Maria Rilke says, that we will live our way someday into the answer, and not only live a life of peace, but encounter the God of peace every step along the way.

7.

Intimate Prayer

As we imagine ourselves with God, grace engulfs us and we are drawn deeper into the divine presence. We feel God's love for us personally. Our affections are stirred. Over time, we are drawn into an intimate relationship with God. Intimate prayer then becomes the basis for all our other relationships.

A lasting intimate relationship with the God of peace and the whole human family is the goal of prayer, of life itself. As we enter into intimate peace with God, our true selves are revealed. We come alive. We accept ourselves as broken, but find ourselves whole. Perhaps for the first time, our true identities as daughters and sons of God, sisters and brothers to one another, are revealed. In this intimate place, we are the people we were created to be. We know why we exist. We rejoice in God, and God becomes the center of our lives, the inspiration of our actions.

Being touched by God is like falling in love. Our lives are turned upside down. We want to spend all our time with our Beloved. Prayer becomes our quality time with our significant other. We seek private time with our beloved God as often as we can. With each passing day, each passing year, we move farther beyond words to the prayer of intimate presence and affection. God embraces us. Our spirits unite. We are re-created, restored in ways we never dreamed possible.

God wants to be with us. God has done everything to share love with humanity, with each of us individually and all of us collectively. The story of Jesus reveals this. Jesus reaches out to everyone around him, but they reject him. He invites everyone to share his loving relationship with God, but they respond by mocking and rejecting him. He calls God his loving Father and teaches how God wants us to live as loving sisters and brothers; the crowds turn on him. He protests the systemic violence of institutionalized religion, declares God's love, and demands nonviolence; they plot to kill him. Even as his own friends betray him, he offers them the Eucharist, offering to be their food and drink, the ultimate act of reconciling love.

Jesus holds nothing back. The more people reject him and hurt him, the more he responds with love and forgiveness. In our intimate prayer, this same Jesus, alive and risen, draws close. He simply longs to be with us as we are, to share his life of love.

We can think of Jesus throughout our day-to-day lives. We read about him. We study his life. We try to imitate him. But in prayer, we feel his living presence within us. We talk to him. We listen to him. We dwell quietly in his abiding love.

As we look into the eyes of Jesus, imagine his wounded hands welcoming us, and embrace him, love overwhelms us. Grace takes over. Our hearts burn with love. We adore Christ. In intimate prayer with Christ, we forget ourselves and become fully attentive to the Holy One. God's divine love meets our human affections. We rest in that love. Slowly we learn to reach out to others with that same love and affection.

John's Gospel explains the inviting love of Jesus. "Whoever has my commandments and observes them is the one who loves me. And whoever loves me will be loved by my God and I will love them and reveal myself to them" (John 14:21). "Whoever loves me will keep my word and my God will love them, and we will come to them and make our dwelling with them" (14:23). "Remain in me as I remain in you" (15:4). "As God loves me, so I also love you. Remain in my love. If you keep my commandments, you will remain in my love, just as I have kept my God's commandments and remain in God's love" (15:9–10). Even to the hour of his execution, Jesus invited all to share in his intimate love with God.

For twenty years, I have struggled to take time each day for prayer, not just vocal prayers like "the Lord's Prayer," or communal prayer like the Eucharist, or "lectio divina," the reflective reading of the scriptures, but especially quiet, intimate prayer. Sometimes, I find myself at some deep place beyond words, where I feel the abiding presence of Jesus. Then, my heart burns with a desire to stay there forever. I know I cannot manufacture such feelings. This is a grace. In such moments, I forget myself. Distracting thoughts disappear. I am centered in Christ's peace. Jesus is at least as real to me as those physically in the same room.

These moments are intensely personal. At the same time, they compose the center of my spiritual life and I long to share them. I am convinced that if we all took time to dwell in Jesus' loving presence, our hearts would be converted, our lives would be changed, and we would actively demonstrate nonviolence and compassionate love toward the whole human race. We would love one another as Jesus instructs, because we would understand that we are truly loved.

That this unconditional love is available to every human being gives me hope. Each one of us can practice intimate prayer at any time. All we have to do is quiet ourselves down, open our hearts to God, offer ourselves to God, accept God's unconditional love for us, love God with all our hearts, and rest in this intimacy. We can imagine resting our heads on God's shoulder, or lying prostrate at the feet of the risen Christ, or breathing in the Holy Spirit. The point is to adore God, to be lost in love for God. As this intimate relationship grows in our hearts and we remain faithful to our Beloved, we will be able to love and serve others in peace because our lives spring for this intimate love.

Shortly after arriving in India in the late 1940s, a young Albanian Sister of Loreto was traveling by train across the countryside to a meeting. She was alone, leaning against the window, enjoying, as she later described it, "intimate prayer with God," when she heard an inner voice telling her to go and serve the poorest of the poor. Mother Teresa's new mission of charity grew from that "intimate prayer."

In the 1980s, Henri Nouwen sought her out for advice. "When you spend one hour a day adoring your Lord and never do anything that you know is wrong, you will be fine," she said. "Mother Teresa's answer was like a flash of lightning in my darkness," Nouwen later wrote. "I suddenly knew the truth of myself." In all his subsequent books, he urged us to live the "life of the beloved," to stay centered in this intimate love, and to adore our Lord.

Despite the failings of churches and other religious institutions, despite the horrors of world violence, the God of peace waits patiently for each of us, offering a loving embrace, seeking intimacy with us. What history's saints and peacemakers teach us is that there is nothing to fear! Our God loves us! All that is required of us is to welcome God's love, to receive it, to remain in it, and to share it with one another. All we have to do is let God love us. As we do, we will be filled with a deep peace.

8.

Mindfulness

The Vietnamese Buddhist monk and antiwar activist Thich Nhat Hanh teaches that mindfulness is also key to the life of peace. If we want to dwell in peace, Nhat Hanh explains, we need to be present to the moment we are living in here and now. If we think of the past or look ahead to the future, we miss the present moment, and with that, the opportunity of deep, contemplative peace. If we live in the present moment, however, we remain centered and enter into God's perfect peace.

As a means of prayer, mindfulness teaches us to attend to the sound and rhythm of our breathing. We consciously slow down and notice each breath we take in and each breath we let out. With each breath we inhale, we breathe in the spirit of peace. With each breath we exhale, we offer back the spirit of peace to humanity. By attending to our breath, we dwell in the present moment. We are fully alive and conscious of the life within us. We accept all things, let go of all things, and radiate the peace of God's own spirit. We stand detached from all things, free. We remain calm, quiet, as gentle as our breathing.

Mindfulness allows us to experience peace. With the discipline of contemplation, mindfulness opens up the possibility of peace as a way of life.

The sun is setting and a fog bank rolls in over the ocean as I write these words in a hermitage on Block Island off the coast of Rhode Island. The sky blends with the ocean and fog to create an atmosphere of peaceful beauty. I am surrounded by pine trees and woods inhabited by birds, several deer, one magnificent quail (who keeps watch over the hermitage at sunset each evening), a pond, and directly before me, down a cliff, the awesome Atlantic. All is peace. The silence of this solitude is soothing. I breathe in, with gratitude for the gift of peace. I breathe out, sharing the spirit of peace. I breathe in the spirit of life. I breathe out, sharing that spirit with all humanity.

Alert in this sacred space, I meditate on Christ. I imagine him here with me. I listen to his voice. He speaks words of love. He is vulnerable, fully attentive. He is my peace. I smile. I breathe.

As I practice mindfulness, I am not undertaking my own private spirituality. I am not forsaking the world or turning my back on action for justice and peace. On the contrary, I am helping the nonviolent transformation of the world led by the spirit of peace.

As I breathe in, I am conscious of humanity also breathing. I realize my position as a member of the entire human family. I enter more deeply into the spirit of nonviolence. I am taken up into God's own breath. I transcend my self, shedding violence, letting go of worries. I am conscious of all humanity, living, breathing, born, suffering, dying. In our breath, we are one. Dwelling in the spirit of peace, attending to the Christ of peace, I am formed into an instrument of peace, at the service of suffering humanity.

This afternoon, I drove to the other side of the island to walk the rocky beach and watch the fog roll in. Turning down a dirt road on my way to the beach, my car hit a rock. The front tire exploded and the side of the car skid up an embankment. I feared the car would tip over, but suddenly it crashed back down to the ground. My right hand smashed against the rearview mirror. The car stopped and I took a deep breath. I got out of the car.

The fog quietly rolled in.

I found a rock to secure the rear tire, jacked up the front of the car, removed the damaged tire, and put on the spare. The hand-pump jack was hard to operate, and the metal rod that jacks the car kept falling from its slot, knocking my hand against the rocky road beneath. Looking at my scratched knuckles, I breathed in. I breathed out. I sat by the abandoned road along the shore of the island, breathing in, breathing out, in, out—at peace.

There I sat, fully present, changing a tire. I felt calm. I found myself smiling as I lowered the car, one twist of the jack at a time. When the car was ready, I discovered that the new tire was also flat! I laughed. I smiled. I looked up at the sky. The fog continued to roll in slowly. *This is a moment of peace*, I told myself. The car and I limped into town for repair at the island auto shop. I took a deep breath. I smiled.

I rarely feel so centered, but I realized then and there that if I try to be mindful, I can be at peace no matter what the day brings.

Mindfulness is an utterly simple practice, and yet one of the most demanding, trying disciplines in the life of contemplative peacemaking. Whatever my day-to-day work brings—speaking, organizing, traveling, meetings, friends, family, community—mindfulness offers a path back to the present moment, to the peace of God.

The world does not need more chaos. The world needs peace. We cannot offer peace to the world if we lack inner peace ourselves, and mindfulness is a key ingredient to daily inner peace.

Whether in a hermitage, a busy office, a crowded subway, a prison cell, or a war zone, mindfulness can help us experience in the present the peace we long for. As a means of contemplative prayer, mindfulness enables us to be fully present to all around us.

In a mindless world of violence, mindfulness makes all the difference. It transforms our inner peace into radiant public action. In this light, we see enough to take the next step, and walk forward in our war-torn world offering the wisdom of peace.

II.

The Heights of Peace:

The Public Journey

There is no way to peace. Peace is the way.

A. J. MUSTE

An individual has not started living until he or she can rise above the narrow confines of his or her individualistic concerns to the broader concerns of all humanity.

MARTIN LUTHER KING, JR.

I'm a nonviolent soldier. In place of weapons of violence, you have to use your mind, your heart, your sense of humor, every faculty available to you because no one has the right to take the life of another human being.

JOAN BAEZ

We have to make truth and nonviolence not matters for mere individual practice but for practice for groups and communities and nations. That at any rate is my dream. I shall live and die trying to realize it.

MAHATMA GANDHI

9.

The Vision of Peace

Over the last twenty years, while meeting suffering people across the world, I have made a great discovery. Behind the barricades of Belfast, in the mountain villages of Guatemala and El Salvador, on remote islands of the Philippines, on the streets of Baghdad, Hebron, Port-au-Prince, Harlem, and Washington, D.C., in the countless jails, hospitals, shelters, soup kitchens, and death rows I have visited—wherever I go, whomever I meet, whatever eyes I look into—I see another child of God. Here is another sister, another brother.

How we live in the world depends on how we see ourselves and the world itself.

If we believe life has no ultimate meaning, that the world will always be in chaos, and that we can get ahead of others by whatever means necessary, then we will self-destruct along with the world. A self-fulfilling prophecy.

But if we believe life has purpose, that the Creator is a God of peace, and that we are called to plumb its depths, then life and our contribution to humanity take on a redemptive potential.

If we want to live in peace with all humanity, we have to see with the eyes of peace. Then, we will begin to envision what Martin Luther King, Jr., called "the beloved community," what Jesus called, "the reign of God."

A life of peace begins with the simplest and most basic truth: We are all equal. Every human being is equal to every other human being. We are all sisters and brothers, all children of the God of peace. This vision is fundamental reality. All life is sacred. Everything we do or say comes from this vision.

If we kill other human beings, we destroy our very sisters and brothers. Once we truly realize the essential unity of all life, we can never hurt or kill another human being, much less wage war, build nuclear weapons, or allow millions of human beings to starve to death each year.

The culture of violence around us insists that all are not equal. Some people, often many people, it claims, are outsiders, enemies, not human. They can be marginalized. They can be killed. Once we dehumanize another, then we can kill and wage war.

Unfortunately, history, including our own recent history, is filled with examples. Through colonialism, we massacred the native peoples of North America until they were forced into their "reservations." Through racism and the legacy of slavery, the Ku Klux Klan dehumanized, terrorized, and lynched African Americans across the South. In Guatemala, U.S.—funded government death squads murdered over 100,000 indigenous people during the 1980s because their language, class, and culture were different from those in power. By denying our shared humanity with the Vietnamese people, we were able to drop millions of tons of bombs on them during the Vietnam War, killing over two million sisters and brothers over ten years. Such dehumanization, marginalization, and mass murder continue today in over thirty-five wars.

The culture around us teaches that a vision of peace is just a dream, and that the only way to live in the real world is to make as much money as you can, acquire power, and dominate as much as possible.

Instead of a culture of inclusion, we live in a culture of division. Instead of a culture of justice, we live in a culture of injustice. Instead of a culture of compassion and forgiveness, we live in a culture of revenge and retaliation. Instead of a culture of nonviolence, we live in a culture of violence. Instead of a culture of peace, we live in a culture of war.

If we want to move toward a culture of peace and nonviolence, we will have to open our eyes, see with new vision, and recognize every human being as our very own sister and brother. This vision of peace is the center of the world's religions and a spirituality of peace and nonviolence.

As we begin to see the world through the lens of nonviolence, we are not only appalled by the world's violence, we commit ourselves to ending it. We begin to resist wars, violence, and other injustices, and promote peace, justice, and active nonviolence for all of humanity.

More and more people share our vision. Scales fall from our eyes. Weapons fall from our hands. Suddenly the great truth hidden since the creation of the world is revealed: We are *already* reconciled to one another and to God. We are already one.

We are transformed forever. From that moment forward, we can reach out to befriend every one we see, every human being on earth, especially the suffering, the ostracized, the poor, the enemy, because we know everyone as our sister and brother.

This vision is easy to accept if we but open our eyes to the sanctity of life and the equality of the human family. Living out that vision for the rest of our days is more difficult. The culture will insist that we are blind. Centuries of war and violence have convinced us that some, but not all, are equal, and thus some can be legally disposed. The culture will claim who can live and who can die. If we insist on the truth of our vision of humanity, and say what we see and what it means to us, then we will have to live it out, even in the face of cultural opposition. From now on, that vision will tell us that everyone gets to live.

We humbly go forward to do the works of peace, to not only stop our complicity in the suffering of humanity but to contribute to the world's nonviolent transformation. Despite the culture's blindness and its insistence that human life can be taken, we will never again condone violence. From now on, we will choose the life of peace.

10.

Choosing Peace

To live a life of peace, we must practice peace with all we meet, indeed, with the whole world. To practice this publicly, we consciously reject the chaos around us and steadfastly choose peace. Once we make that choice, a whole new journey begins.

Throughout our lives, we are invited to make choices. Most of our energy is spent deciding over insignificant matters. But as we push beyond these mundane choices, we come upon eternal questions: What does it mean to be human? What shall I do with my life? How do I prepare for death? How can I know God?

As we contemplate these questions, we find the great choices opening before us: whether or not to accept that God is God; whether or not to live in peace.

Choosing peace invites our daily participation in the greatest spiritual and moral struggle facing humanity, the life-long struggle of nonviolence.

If we fully choose peace, we can change the world. A life-long pursuit of peace promises not only inner adventure, struggling with the forces of chaos and violence (the deepest meaning for our existence), but the possibility of affecting the very course of history.

Whether we radiate quiet peace like a Buddhist monk or capture the world's imagination like Mahatma Gandhi, a life of peace bears fruit for humanity.

I remember the day I was confronted with my great choice. In June 1982, I was twenty-one, living with my parents in Washington, D.C., about to enter the Society of Jesus, the Jesuits, a worldwide community of Catholic priests. I decided that before I committed my life to following Jesus, I wanted to go to Israel and see for myself the land where Jesus lived and died.

My plans for a typical pious pilgrimage were shattered, though. As I was boarding the plane to Tel Aviv, Israel was invading Lebanon. I was heading into a war. Stepping off the plane in Tel Aviv, I was greeted by armed soldiers who searched me, questioned me, and finally waved me on with machine guns. For the next five weeks, I wandered through the Holy

Land, visiting sacred sites, talking with Israelis, and reading the Gospels. But the reality of the war shocked me, terrified me, and changed my life.

After exploring every corner of Jerusalem, Bethlehem, and Nazareth, I spent my last week camping out by myself along the Sea of Galilee. It was beautiful. Each morning, I rose with the sun, swam in the cool water, and meditated on the teachings of Jesus, who lived and worked along the north shore of Galilee, in the village of Capernaum.

Every day, I climbed a little hill on the north shore near the ruins of Capernaum to pray in the Chapel of the Beatitudes. The eight-sided chapel is surrounded by palm trees, cactus, and green shrubs. There I would sit in silence and read the words of scripture engraved on the walls. I would walk out onto the balcony and look out at the blue sea. The view was breathtaking. For hours, I would read the Sermon on the Mount, look at the sea, and pray for guidance.

As my time in Galilee drew to a close, I made one last visit to the Chapel of the Beatitudes. I sat alone in the chapel reading the words written on the eight windows:

Blessed are the poor in spirit. Theirs is the reign of heaven.
Blessed are those who mourn. They shall be comforted.
Blessed are the meek. They shall inherit the land.

Blessed are those who hunger and thirst for justice. They
 shall be satisfied.
Blessed are the merciful. They shall be shown mercy.
Blessed are the pure in heart. They shall see God.
Blessed are the peacemakers. They shall be called sons and
 daughters of God.
Blessed are those who are persecuted for the sake of justice.
 Theirs is the reign of heaven.
Blessed are you when others revile you and persecute you
 and utter all kinds of evil against you falsely on my ac-
 count. Rejoice and be glad, for your reward is great in
 heaven. (Matthew 5:3–12)

"I say to you, love your enemies, and pray for those who persecute you, that you may be children of your heavenly God, for
God makes God's sun rise on the bad and the good, and causes
rain to fall on the just and the unjust. Be compassionate as your
heavenly God is compassionate." (Matthew 5:44–45)

Suddenly, the words of Jesus hit me as if for the first time.
As a light went on, I thought to myself, *Oh my God, I think he's
serious!*

I walked onto the balcony and looked out at the sea, the
distant mountains, the clear blue sky.

"Are you trying to tell me something, God?" I said aloud,

looking up at the sky. "Do you want even me to become a peacemaker, to hunger and thirst for justice, to love my enemies?

"Okay, God," I said out loud. "I promise to live the life of peace, to live out these Beatitudes for the rest of my life—on one condition: if you give me a sign!"

With that, I put my fist down on the stone wall, proud of my conditional commitment.

Just then, two Israeli war jets fell through the sky, breaking the sound barrier with sonic booms, over the Sea of Galilee, flying low, straight toward me! I ducked instinctively. They raced directly over me and the Chapel of the Beatitudes and, seconds later, dropped several bombs along the border between Israel and Lebanon.

I rose and looked back up at the sky.

"Okay, God," I said, shaking. "I promise to dedicate myself to peace and justice for the rest of my life—and I'll never ask for a sign again!"

As a Christian, I committed myself to live according to the Beatitudes, the Sermon on the Mount, and Jesus' peacemaking life. That meant, like Jesus, I would be required to find inner peace and publicly oppose violence and war, pursuing a world of peace with justice for all.

The next day, I traveled to the Israeli border, to the town of Queryat Shemona. There I saw tanks, jeeps, and heavy military equipment roll into Lebanon. Armed soldiers milled about. War, in its abrupt contrast to the message of the Chapel of the Beatitudes, shocked me and confirmed my choice. Two weeks later, I entered the Jesuit Novitiate, a Catholic seminary in Wernersville, Pennsylvania, for two years of prayer and religious training.

Now, twenty years later, I realize that we have to choose to live in peace every day of our lives. We don't have to go to the Middle East to see war or to hear Christ's plea for peace.

Every moment offers us God's invitation to live in God's own peace. Wherever we are, we can reject violence and war, and take up the exciting journey by proclaiming God's reign of peace here on earth.

The challenge is to start the journey, to stay faithful, and to delve into a life of peace. Though there will be many days when the journey will seem futile, daunting, even hopeless, over time we come to realize that the journey itself is the life of peace! All we have to do is choose to take up that journey and stay faithful.

"All the way to heaven is heaven," St. Catherine of Siena once said. Once we make the choice to live a life of peace, we will receive all the direction we need.

11.

Active Nonviolence

If the twentieth century has taught us anything, it's that wars never solve problems. Violence never breaks the chain of violence. "Returning violence for violence only multiplies violence, adding deeper darkness to a night already devoid of stars," Martin Luther King, Jr., said. "Darkness cannot drive out darkness, only light can do that. Hate cannot drive out hate; only love can do that."

In 1982, when I entered the Jesuit Novitiate, I was on fire to follow the peacemaking Jesus. I stayed up late talking with my classmates about our lives, our God, our hopes for the world. I read every book I could find about justice and peace. I meditated, read the scriptures, and went on long walks alone.

As I studied the lives of saints and peacemakers like Dorothy Day, Dr. King, and others, I came to the conclusion that nonviolence is at the heart of spiritual life.

There is growing interest today in "spirituality." Some define it as "the way we live our lives." Others explain it as how we define our inner search for meaning. Many use the term to sum up our relationship with God. But the problem is that most people have privatized their spirituality, and think solely in terms of a vertical relationship with God, as if our relationship with God exempts us from our responsibility to the human race. We are all searching for God, for meaning in life, for fulfillment. But if we allow violence into our hearts, then we are not practicing an authentic spirituality. This common misunderstanding of the spiritual life has led us to self-absorption and selfish indifference toward suffering humanity. Authentic spirituality includes compassionate action. It is rooted in nonviolence.

Gandhi first coined the term "nonviolence" to describe *satyagraha*, the force of truth as active love. Nonviolence begins when we renounce violence, from subtle inner violence to complicity in the world's wars and systemic injustice. Nonviolence insists upon life, liberty, and justice for everyone. But no matter how noble the struggle for peace and justice, the spirituality of nonviolence holds that there is no cause for which one can kill. To live in nonviolence, we cannot hurt others, kill others, wage war, or remain silent in the face of systemic injustice. We must refuse to cooperate with the world's violence.

But nonviolence is much more than the renunciation of violence. It encompasses unconditional, compassionate love, rooted in truth and justice. It is the social, spiritual force of life itself, God in humanity, making us one. In this spirit of love and truth, we radiate peace and passionately pursue justice for all, especially the disenfranchised and oppressed.

Nonviolence, as Gandhi taught, means disassociating ourselves from every inclination to violence, internally and interpersonally. It means actively, publicly engaging in a peaceful pursuit of truth and social justice for all humanity. It requires dedicating our lives to promoting the fullness of life for every human being.

But here's the catch: Nonviolence confronts systemic injustice with active love, but refuses to retaliate with further violence under any circumstances. In order to halt the vicious cycle of violence, it requires a willing acceptance of suffering and death rather than inflicting suffering or death on anyone else.

The art of nonviolence lies in the mastery of dying, not killing. Instead of nailing others to the cross, we are willing to accept the cross ourselves, like Jesus—until humanity is worn down and won over, until no one is ever crucified again, until a new world without violence or war is born.

Nonviolence invites us to embrace the world's suffering, like Jesus dying on the cross, saying, "The violence stops here, in my body." We would offer our last breath with love in our hearts and forgiveness on our lips, but we would not strike back or hurt others in order simply to protect ourselves. Nonviolence requires sacrifice, love, forgiveness, and truth. It is the path to solidarity with humanity and with God. While it takes up the cause of suffering humanity to the point of risking one's life for the poor and marginalized, it insists that there is no cause, no movement, no struggle worth killing for, no matter how just.

If we want to live in peace, we have to renounce our violence and embrace nonviolence as a way of life. As we choose a life of peace, we end the wars raging within our own hearts and root out every trace of violence. We let go of violent language, habits, manners, and jobs, and cease whatever actions, however subtle, that hurt or threaten others.

This reexamination of our lives will expose our past injury of others. We will want to reverse whatever harm we have caused others by apologizing, offering restitution, pursuing healing, and reconciling with everyone. Through humble, loving service, we try to bring peace to everyone for the rest of our lives.

As we test the waters of nonviolence, we come face to face with the sufferings of the poor. As we meet those who have been rejected, disenfranchised, and injured by the culture of violence, we can try our best to alleviate their suffering. The desire to alleviate human suffering caused by injustice can lead us into the horrific realities of war and global economic oppression. The more we see of violence, the more we can engage in active nonviolence to promote justice and peace.

For many, the journey to peace begins with small acts of charity to the poor. As we engage in good charity works, we encounter the marginalized, make friends with them, and learn why they are suffering injustice. As we scratch the surface of injustices imposed on low-income peoples, we may find ourselves asking why our nation can not feed the starving, educate children, and relieve such widespread misery. We learn that our nation instead spends billions upon billions of dollars funding not programs to serve suffering humanity but weapons of mass destruction. This may lead us to study disarmament and the abolition of war. As we pursue the urgent work of nuclear and conventional disarmament and resisting wars, it becomes more and more obvious that a future of peace can only be found through the wisdom of active nonviolence. And so, like Gandhi, Dr. King, and Dorothy Day, we may begin to advocate nonviolence as the core of life.

I know hundreds of extraordinary people who live ordinary lives of active nonviolence. I think of Richard Deats at the Fellowship of Reconciliation, who has been teaching nonviolence, joining demonstrations, and building community all his life. I think of Lynn Fredriksson, Washington director of the East Timor Action Network, who has given her life to quiet, active nonviolence for struggling nations of the world. I think of Kathy Boylan, a mother and grandmother, who runs a house of hospitality for the homeless, and organizes regular prayer vigils and demonstrations against war, injustice, and nuclear weapons. Though the culture does not honor these practitioners of nonviolence, they and thousands of others live honorable lives dedicated to peace.

For many Christians, nonviolence is no longer a pious option or a political tactic. It is the key to understanding Jesus. The only things we know for sure about Jesus are that he did not kill and he opposed violence of any kind. He rejected violence of both oppressor and oppressed. He taught a third way—active nonviolent resistance to evil. He urged his followers to love God, to love one's self, to love one's neighbors, and most radical of all, to love even one's enemies.

When I was a Jesuit novice, just back from the Middle East, I knew that the spiritual-political teachings of Jesus could literally transform the world. We cannot kill, period. We cannot wage war. We cannot make nuclear weapons. We cannot threaten to bomb others. We cannot execute, torture, shoot, stab, hang, gas, or incinerate people. We are commanded to love every being on earth, even those who oppose us or seek to kill us. We must win them over through loving kindness and forgive over and over. If we can love our enemies, instead of threatening to kill or bomb them, we can stop our enmity, transform our relationships, and create harmony and reconciliation with all of humanity.

During those quiet, reflective years in the Jesuit Novitiate, I also learned that nonviolence is not passive. It is an active, creative way of life that plumbs the depths of the heart, transforming violence into deep inner peace. In the Pennsylvania countryside, my friends and I talked about nonviolence for hours on end. We decided to fast one day a week, pray together for nuclear disarmament, and systematically discuss the writings of the great peacemakers.

But that was not enough. We attended classes on the scriptures. We learned about the Jesuit mission to promote justice for the poor and the religious vows of poverty, chastity, and obedience in community. Several days a week, we drove into nearby towns and served people in hospitals, soup kitchens, prisons, and shelters. I worked at a school for mentally and physically disabled children. Our two years of study, prayer, and reflection were leading to the profession of our perpetual vows.

At the time, I was reading Louis Fisher's brilliant biography, *The Life of Mahatma Gandhi*, and discovered that Gandhi professed fourteen vows, including vows of poverty, chastity, truth-telling, vegetarianism, and nonviolence. Inspired by his disciplined commitment, I decided to profess a similar vow of nonviolence as a way to focus my commitment to Jesus' active, suffering love.

After months of preparation, after we professed our vows of poverty, chastity, and obedience, three friends and I also professed a vow of nonviolence. We wanted to formalize our commitment to the spiritual journey of peace. We wrote the words as a sacred pledge to become God's instruments of peace. "Trusting in your infinite goodness and mercy, before the cross of Jesus, I vow perpetual nonviolence in fulfillment of the command of Jesus to love everyone and in imitation of his holy life and death," we said. "Make us instruments of your peace, channels of your nonviolent love," we prayed. This liturgy was not a culmination of our spiritual lives; it was just the beginning.

If violence is forgetting or ignoring who we are, nonviolence is remembering and recalling every day of our lives that we are all equal, all sisters and brothers, all children of God, all already reconciled to one another and God. It means living our lives from this basic spiritual reality. Nonviolence begins within us, within our own war-torn hearts. All of the world's violence, war, and nuclear weapons are rooted in our own hearts. The journey of nonviolence, Gandhi taught, is a journey of the heart. If we want to be peacemakers and activists, we have to plunge to the inner depths of nonviolence. We must disarm our own hearts so that we can cease our own violence, ego, and domination and begin to offer something more positive to the world. We must spend our lives becoming nonviolent people.

Once we truly understand we are one with every other being, we cannot harm another. Nonviolence is creative love in action on behalf of suffering humanity. Nonviolence demands resistance to evil, but does not permit the use of evil means. Instead, we utilize the arsenal of nonviolence, including prayer, fasting, letter-writing campaigns, education, public hearings, negotiations, vigils, boycotts, demonstrations, and civil disobedience.

If we are truly practicing nonviolence as a way of life, living out the sacredness of life, we are never justified in using violence. We realize that there are no just wars. War is always morally wrong. Because we believe in the God of peace, we know there is always a way to avoid war. Creative nonviolent alternatives can never be exhausted. There are always further negotiations and dialogue, or active nonviolent resistance, even

on a massive level. Instead of bombing Yugoslavia to stop eth-
nic cleansing in Kosovo, for example, we could have supported
the nonviolent resistance movements in Kosovo and the
democracy movements in Yugoslavia, as the people of Kosovo
begged us to for years. The U.S./NATO bombings in the Spring
of 1999 killed over five thousand civilians, including thousands
of refugees we professed to help. Our war-making completely
destroyed Yugoslavia, strengthened the fascist Serbian government for a while, flooded the land with depleted uranium,
pushed the United Nations aside when international peacemakers were critically needed, and made billions of dollars for
U.S. weapons manufacturers. Worse still, it sowed seeds of war
and division. Only active nonviolence and civil disobedience
on a massive scale brought about a new government for Yugoslavia in the Fall of 2000.

As Dr. King taught, nonviolence seeks to defeat injustice,
not people. It recognizes that evildoers are also victims and are
not evil people. It liberates the oppressed and the oppressors.
It constantly wins friendship and understanding, resulting in
redemption and reconciliation, not resentment and revenge.
Nonviolence refuses hate. It calls for love of everyone. Jesus offered the ultimate teaching on nonviolence: Instead of killing
your enemies, love your enemies.

Love in action has the power to transform even the most
divided community. "Unearned suffering is redemptive," Dr.

King taught. Through the power of suffering love, opponents can be won over and the truth of justice and reconciliation revealed. When King led the demonstrators in Birmingham in the Spring of 1963 to march to break segregation laws, the police unleashed dogs on children and firemen used water as a weapon, but the demonstrators did not strike back. They maintained a spirit of disciplined, nonviolent love. Their suffering in truth was revealed not only to Birmingham but the whole world. In one dramatic moment, while police chief Bull Connor screamed, firemen disobeyed his orders and put down their hoses. Marchers walked peacefully through their midst, and forged a new opening to peace, justice and civil rights. Their dramatic witness helped pave the way for new civil rights legislation as well as the historic March on Washington that August.

The goal of nonviolence, according to Dr. King, is the revelation of "the beloved community." Gandhi believed God will reign on earth when everyone realizes nonviolence. That is our life mission—to convert each other and all of humanity to the wisdom of the practice of nonviolence.

Life continuously reveals to us how deep our own violence lies within us. We will never become perfectly nonviolent because we have been thoroughly socialized into a culture of violence. But we can turn away from violence, seek inner peace, practice heartfelt compassion toward others, and publicly participate in the world's nonviolent transformation.

"My optimism rests on my belief in the infinite possibilities of the individual to develop nonviolence," Gandhi concluded. "The more you develop it in your own being, the more infectious it becomes until it overwhelms your surroundings and by and by might oversweep the world. Nonviolence is the greatest and most active force in the world. One person who can express nonviolence in life exercises a force superior to all the forces of brutality."

To live a life of peace is to walk the way of nonviolence. It means taking up the public witness where Gandhi, Dr. King, and other peacemakers left off. As we practice nonviolence, we not only help create a culture of nonviolence, we welcome God's reign of nonviolence in our midst.

12

Public Peacemaking

A life of peace includes not only the private, inner journey to peace of heart, but a lifelong, public journey to
peace for all of humanity. Once we drink from the spiritual
source within us, we want to share that gift with everyone. We
feel compelled to spend our days offering gifts of peace to all
we meet.

Peacemaking is not political like electoral campaigns or
self-centered ambitions for power, but it does require that we
stand up publicly.

In the face of massive cultural violence, silence is complicity. That means, we need to get involved—with a local peace
group, through a religious community, a neighborhood center,
or a national peace organization like the Fellowship of Reconciliation. As more and more ordinary people join together, society will change.

As I read about the lives of great peacemakers while I was in the Jesuit Novitiate, I knew that I, too, had to speak out for peace and disarmament. I saw how the great spiritual and moral leaders of our time broke through their own fears and weaknesses to advocate publicly for peace. Their lives often unexpectedly bore tremendous fruit. I wondered what difference I could make, then I realized success was not necessarily the point. The point was simply to do what I could: to *try* to make peace wherever I went; to hope and pray that God would use my small efforts to aid in something much greater.

A friend and I decided to undertake a series of pseudoscientific public experiments with nonviolence. We had been sent to live and work for six months at Georgetown University in Washington, D.C., in the spring of 1984 to experience life in the Jesuit community. I was assigned to start a tutoring and social program to bring Georgetown students together with young Salvadoran refugee boys and girls, who at that time were entering the D.C. public school system at a rate of fifty per week. The program took off. Within months, nearly two hundred college students were volunteering to work with an even greater number of Salvadoran teenagers. The Georgetown students, we discovered, were eager to do some concrete community service, but the young Salvadorans were so friendly and excited to meet us that they immediately won even more over. Word quickly spread about these extraordinary young people who had suffered so much from their country's civil war. Suddenly hundreds of Georgetown students wanted to help out the young Salvadorans. It was a concrete way each one of us could connect with the suffering people of Central America and offer a hand of friendship, healing, and reconciliation.

Soon, however, my attention turned to the Pentagon and its preparations for war. I watched our country actively waging war against impoverished peoples in Nicaragua and El Salvador. I heard how priests and nuns, even Archbishop Oscar Romero, were assassinated for their opposition to the U.S.–backed military repression. I made my first weekend retreat with the Jesuit peacemaker Father Daniel Berrigan, and felt inspired by Dan's biblical reflections calling for a public stand for peace.

With another novice I concocted a plan to visit the Pentagon every Wednesday morning during Lent to engage Pentagon employees in conversation about disarmament. In the spirit of Gandhi, we called our Lenten campaign our own "experiments in nonviolence."

The night before our first vigil, we decided we would wear our clerical garb and approach the employees entering the building. We would ask them to return home, pray for peace, and quit working for war.

It was a ridiculous proposition.

But what did we have to lose?

"We can't be passive about this," my friend argued. "We need to plead with these people in no uncertain words, for the love of God, to stop plotting the mass murder of other human beings and the destruction of the planet!"

"No, no, no! We're people of peace," I retorted, with an air of self-righteous assurance, as if I were the great expert about how to promote peace with Pentagon generals. "We will not be angry, violent, or judgmental. We will not yell or raise our voice. We will simply ask them to go home and work for peace, and we will do so in a spirit of peace."

Our first morning at the Pentagon, Ash Wednesday, 1984, was bitterly cold. As we approached the massive stone building—the largest in the world—I was overcome with images of war. Here before my eyes was the greatest center for the study and practice of mass murder in the history of the world! And everyone was acting so normal. It seemed to me as if humanity had gone insane. I felt sick to my stomach, as I did when I toured Dachau years earlier.

A black limousine pulled up. Out stepped a general in ribbons and medals. I ran up to him, arms flailing, begging, yelling, "For the love of God, go home and stop preparing to wage war! For the love of God, stop preparing to kill!"

The general and his aides brushed me aside. They didn't even blink. They ignored us and walked past us, as if they were used to such opposition. My friend came running up to restrain me. "Stop it, John!" he pleaded. "I thought you said we were to be peaceful and nonviolent."

It was a revelation. All the anger and violence within me had surfaced, and I saw the face of war not in the Pentagon general but in myself! A great lesson. I had much to learn.

Each week we tried a different experiment in nonviolence, from silent prayer to leafletting, from holding antiwar posters to reading the Sermon on the Mount to thousands of Pentagon employees walking past us. As I engaged the Pentagon employees in a call to peace, I began to hear that call myself, as if for the first time.

My first weeks of public peacemaking—while totally insignificant and ineffective to the world—transformed my own life. They culminated in my first act of civil disobedience that Easter, when I walked by myself to the Pentagon. I sat down quietly in a doorway, reading the Sermon on the Mount. Immediately I was surrounded by a dozen police officers who listened quietly for fifteen minutes as I read and prayed. Then I was arrested, booked, and released a few hours later. A few weeks later at trial, I was sentenced to thirty days in jail, but the judge suspended the sentence.

My public journey for peace had begun.

Since those transforming days, I have joined nonviolent campaigns for peace and disarmament across the country. I have organized, lobbied, spoken out, demonstrated, and been arrested in civil disobedience actions at the U.S. Capitol; White House; Strategic Air Command Base in Omaha, Nebraska; Trident submarine bases in Connecticut and Georgia; Riverside Research Institute in New York City; West Point; the Nevada Test Site; Livermore Nuclear Weapons Laboratories; Concord Naval Weapons Station; the School of the Americas; and U.S. federal buildings in San Francisco and Los Angeles.

When the United States began bombing Yugoslavia in the spring of 1999, I helped organize a coalition of peace organizations to speak out against both the genocidal violence of the Serbian military, and the U.S. and NATO bombing that obliterated Yugoslavia and killed thousands of civilians, including refugees. As the bombing continued, several of us asked to meet with President Clinton. When he refused, twenty-six of us, including Bishop Thomas Gumbleton of Detroit, knelt in the White House driveway and prayed for an end to the killing.

Our action was peaceful, prayerful, and public. Before we engaged in our nonviolent protest, I spoke at a rally in Lafayette Park about the urgent moral duty to stop the killing, as I had done a few days earlier on National Public Radio's *All Things Considered*. "A few weeks ago, after the massacre at Columbine High School in Littleton, Colorado, the President said we need to teach our young people to use words, not violence. 'One act of violence is one act too many,' he said. Yet while he tells our young people not to kill or use bombs, the

U.S. continues to kill and drop bombs on Yugoslavia. The White House and the Pentagon teach that killing is morally acceptable, even honorable, and expresses shock when our young people kill one another.

"Today, we call upon the President and NATO to 'use words, not violence.' Instead of bringing peace, we sow seeds of war. Instead of supporting the nonviolence and democracy movements, we crush them. We should pursue diplomatic negotiations, encourage nonviolent resistance and offer to help every single refugee from Kosovo and the whole world."

Unjust means will never bring about just ends, I tried to explain. We cannot fight war crimes by committing war crimes. We can not uphold international law by violating international law. We can not reach moral ends by using immoral means. We can not stop violence by inflicting further violence. We can not teach people who kill not to kill by killing people. Bombings have never ended a war. Wars never solve problems. The U.S. war on Yugoslavia was not only unjust; it was immoral, illegal, and downright impractical. War, genocide, and nuclear weapons can only be stopped through creative, consistent, public, active nonviolence.

We spent most of the day in a D.C. jail cell, talking, praying, laughing, sharing our hopes. We had done what we could. We would have continued the demonstrations, but thank God, the U.S. bombings stopped the next day.

"Don't just stand there: Do something!" In today's world, we all need to get involved, to do something for peace. Not long before he died, I had the chance to speak with United Farm-worker activist César Chávez. I asked him what he thought was the key to peace and justice work. "Public action! Public action! Public action!" he replied. "We all need to act publicly for peace and justice."

Likewise, the opposite is true: "Don't just do something: Stand there!" We need to act publicly, and then remain committed to our actions, to take a permanent stand for the rest of our lives. In that way, we can rest assured that we have done all we could.

13.

Speaking Truth

It is sometimes said that the first casualty of war is truth. In a time of war, lies become commonplace. After a series of wars affecting the whole world, we begin to believe ever greater lies—that nuclear weapons are necessary, that war is justified, that bombing raids are moral, and that in order to protect "our way of life," killing our enemies is our only option.

In a culture of war, the first duty of the peacemaker is to speak the truth of peace. That demands breaking through the lies and insisting despite all opposition on the ancient wisdom of nonviolence.

There are many historical instances of people who have spoken the truth of peace and justice in a time of great turbulence, who suffered for their convictions, and who received recognition for their stand only long after they were dead.

On January 1, 1831, antislavery abolitionist William Lloyd

Garrison published the first edition of *The Liberator*, his groundbreaking abolitionist newspaper. With this paper, he proclaimed to the nation the truth of human equality and denounced the evil of slavery. "I will speak God's truth in its simplicity and power," Garrison declared in the lead editorial that shocked and stirred the nation. "I will be as harsh as truth, and as uncompromising as justice. On this subject I do not wish to think or speak or write with moderation. I am in earnest—I will not equivocate—I will not excuse—I will not retreat a single inch—AND I WILL BE HEARD." That public declaration of the truth shattered the silence that condoned centuries of slavery. It heralded the freedom of millions.[10]

In the face of war and injustice, the truth of peace and justice will not be received with open arms. And yet it must be stated if we are to be people of integrity, if we are ever to live in a culture of nonviolence.

One of my greatest experiences trying to speak the truth publicly occurred in 1994 through 1995 as my friends and I planned to commemorate the fiftieth anniversary of the U.S. atomic bombings of Hiroshima and Nagasaki. We were preparing a summer-long campaign of nonviolence at the Pentagon under the theme, "Remembering the Pain, Repenting the Sin, Reclaiming the Future."

As we began to meet, we read in the newspaper that the Smithsonian's Air and Space Museum was about to put on display the *Enola Gay*, the plane that dropped the atomic bomb on Hiroshima, incinerating 130,000 people instantly and killing untold numbers more from radiation poisoning. After a ten-year, $1-million restoration, it would be unveiled as an historical artifact, along with an extensive exhibit explaining why it was necessary to drop the bomb on Hiroshima.

In other words, the Smithsonian was going to continue the lie that use of nuclear weapons is morally justified, and that the incineration of hundreds of thousands of Japanese sisters and brothers was perfectly reasonable.

From my study, I knew the United States did not need to drop any more bombs to end World War II, despite widespread misconceptions to the contrary. Leading historians and researchers, such as Gar Alperovitz and Kai Bird, have proven that the war was about to end, and that the U.S. government knew it. What the historians are telling us is that the U.S. had the atomic bomb and planned to use it before Japan surrendered in order to show that the U.S., not the Soviet Union, would be recognized as the world's new superpower. The bombings of Hiroshima and Nagasaki were meant to send a strong signal to the Soviet government, not to end the war. They then justified a trillion-dollar nuclear arms race that meant big business for the Pentagon and billions of dollars in profits for its weapons manufacturers.

I wanted very much to try to "experiment with truth," as

Gandhi said. One humid August morning in 1994, I entered the Air and Space Museum, introduced myself to the curator, and asked to read the manuscript for the proposed exhibit. Throughout the previous year, museum staff had met with veterans and military organizations and Pentagon officials more than forty times about the proposed display. I suggested that representatives of national peace organizations should also have the chance to examine the exhibit. Museum officials agreed, and I spent several days at the museum studying the long manuscript.

What I read shocked me. The proposed text offered no mention of the effects of the atomic bombings on human beings. The message of the exhibit was clear: The U.S. had to drop these nuclear weapons. If the U.S. had not dropped these weapons of mass destruction, then the U.S. would have invaded Japan later that year and hundreds of thousands of American soldiers might have died. The incineration of hundreds of thousands of Japanese people "saved the lives of the Americans."

This account of what happened is simply untrue. It is a myth created by the Pentagon to justify the atomic bombings, the Cold War, and the nuclear arms race. Japan was going to surrender. There would not have been a U.S. invasion of Japan. The bombs were used to frighten the U.S.S.R. and gain global hegemony for the U.S.

As I read the text of the exhibit, and mourned the deaths of the Japanese and all victims of war, I asked myself: *How do we break through the myths of war? How do we challenge the lie that nuclear weapons are justifiable, necessary, and at some times, our only option?*

At one point, the curator took me aside, and explained that he had worked on this project for more than a decade and traveled numerous times to Japan. He had given his heart to the project in the hope that it might help Americans come to terms for the first time with the crimes committed in Hiroshima and Nagasaki. "You have no idea the forces arrayed against us," he told me, glancing carefully around the office to see if anyone was listening. He hinted that the exhibit could bring down the whole museum.

I contacted the director's office, and asked if Smithsonian officials would meet with religious leaders and representatives from the peace movement. They agreed.

That September, I brought several leaders from national peace organizations to the Smithsonian for a meeting with Dr. Martin Harwit, museum director, and his staff. They had met the day before with the Air Force Association and the American Legion, who lobbied for an exhibit that would laud the destruction of Hiroshima and Nagasaki and support continued nuclear development Dr. Harwit was eager to hear another perspective.

After he explained the history of the exhibit, we asked Dr. Harwit to rewrite the script. We wanted it framed in a context similar to that used by the United States Holocaust Museum, that we might remember and learn from the atomic bombings of Hiroshima and Nagasaki so that such destruction would never happen again. In particular, we asked that the Smithsonian show the faces of the victims of the U.S. bombings, call for nuclear disarmament, and conclude with a vision of nonviolence as the way to resolve international conflict, again mirroring the Holocaust Museum's message against war and genocide.

Smithsonian officials were open to our perspective, and listened to our suggestions. A few weeks later, we brought in a delegation of historians and scholars from universities around the country. They explained that the atomic bombings were not needed to force Japan's surrender, that they were deliberately dropped to ensure America's superiority over the Soviet Union. Japan was near collapse and ready to surrender if they could retain their emperor, Dr. Barton Bernstein, Professor of History and Director of International Relations at Stanford University, explained. The U.S. knew this. The U.S. had decoded Japanese cables to the Soviets.

"The present script has greatly distorted history, and has disregarded the research of many historians on the subject of Hiroshima and Nagasaki," Dr. Bernstein said. The historians of-

fered a dozen recommendations for revisions to the script, urging that photos and artifacts depict the full extent of human
suffering in Hiroshima and Nagasaki, and that the full history
be told.

The Fellowship of Reconciliation released an open letter
signed by over fifty historians and scholars calling for a new exhibit. "It is most unfortunate that the Smithsonian is becoming
associated with a transparent attempt at historical cleansing,"
the letter stated. "That archival documents and artifacts have
been removed from the planned exhibit under political pressure is an intellectual corruption. The Smithsonian is taking
fastidious care to make sure that each bolt, each gauge and de-
tail of the *Enola Gay* is a perfect reflection of the true artifact.
This stands in extraordinary contrast to the disregard of historical documents and the scholarly literature on the atomic
bombings." While I explained our position to the press, FOR
members flew to Japan to meet with survivors of the atomic
blast and to apologize for the U.S. bombings (and for the exhibit).

Meanwhile, the Air Force Association and the American
Legion mobilized thousands of people to pressure Congress to
censor the museum's proposed revised exhibit. In the end, the
American Legion was so outraged at the Smithsonian for our
meetings and the revised exhibit that they forced the resigna-

tion of Dr. Harwit and the cancellation of the exhibit. They could not accept the truth.

Eventually, the *Enola Gay* was displayed with a one-sentence plaque stating the plane "dropped the atomic bomb that ended the war and saved lives." Congress, veterans' groups, the Pentagon, and the manufacturers of nuclear weapons were relieved. Rush Limbaugh denounced me on his radio program.

"To display the *Enola Gay* without context and without the considerable historical information and interpretation available is to glorify and legitimize the use of nuclear weapons," the Fellowship of Reconciliation concluded.

Our humble effort to speak truth shattered plans to celebrate the fiftieth anniversary of the bombing of Hiroshima as a victory. Public debate about the Smithsonian exhibit revealed that most Americans still have little grasp of what happened at Hiroshima and Nagasaki, where we incinerated hundreds of thousands of people in a flash.[11]

To this day, the U.S. maintains well over 20,000 nuclear weapons. There is no active pursuit of nuclear disarmament, no government intention to abolish them, and no negotiations to protect future generations from danger. Indeed, in the fall of 1999, the U.S. Senate prevented ratification of the Comprehensive Test Ban Treaty. France, Israel, China, England, India, and Pakistan possess nuclear arsenals. Iran, Libya, Algeria,

North Korea, South Korea, Taiwan, Brazil, and Argentina are developing nuclear weapons. The threat of a nuclear accident or use by terrorist groups grows each day.

If we want peace for future generations, we will have to work for a world without nuclear weapons. That means that each one of us will have to speak the truth publicly and denounce war and promote nonviolent alternatives to international crises.

Following the Smithsonian episode, my friends and I organized three weeks of daily public protests for nuclear disarmament at the Pentagon in the summer of 1995. Each evening, we gathered for prayer and a reflection by a leading voice for peace. These actions drew hundreds of people from across the country and culminated on Sunday, August 6, the fiftieth anniversary of the U.S. atomic bombing of Hiroshima, with several thousand people gathering for evening prayer at the National Cathedral in Washington, D.C. The next morning, Father Daniel Berrigan, actor Martin Sheen, and I joined scores of others in a vigil at the Pentagon, and were arrested for blocking the doorways.

"To speak a word of truth," the Brazilian educator Paolo Friere taught, "is to transform the world." The task of the peacemaker is to speak the truth, whether our culture wants to hear it or not. As we speak the truth in a spirit of love and peace, we will realize deeper levels of truth, and begin to understand the great truth of human unity and God's way of non-violence. This proclamation and pursuit of truth will free us from the inevitability of war and the existence of nuclear weapons. But even more importantly, it will lead us to God.

The pursuit of truth ultimately is the pursuit of God. As we pursue truth, we will find God because God is truth. As we go deeper into the truth of reality and plunge the depths of faith in God, we will accept more and more the truth of non-violence and begin to taste the peace that can only come from the God of truth.

14

Live and Let Live

Peace is the ongoing celebration of life. In our vision of peace, we advocate the fullness of life for *every* human being. We mourn the deaths of all victims of violence, but we refuse to retaliate, seek revenge, or further violence in any way. We try to break the downward spiral of violence through active practice of public nonviolence. In order to support life for all, we have to stand up against death.

In the spring of 1988, while I was in Scranton teaching at a Jesuit high school, Pennsylvania announced its first execution in decades. I was crushed by the news. People across the state, many Christian, supported the scheduled murder. My friends and I discussed what we could do.

"What we need is someone like Mother Teresa to intervene for us," I told a friend, a monsignor who worked at the diocesan office.

"Not many people know this," he confided, "but I've led several annual retreats for her. I'm sure she would help."

A light switched on. I began to organize, calling the office of the governor, a widely respected Catholic. I asked if he would receive an appeal from Mother Teresa on behalf of the condemned man. I also notified the press about for the call.

A day before I was going to contact Mother Teresa, a stay of execution was granted. We all rejoiced.

Over the next few years, I arranged Mother Teresa's intervention on behalf of death row inmates on eight separate occasions. Each time, she eagerly offered her support and the prayers of her community to stop the killing and end the death penalty.

In early 1990, while studying at the Jesuit School of Theology in Berkeley, I read in horror of California's impending execution of Robert Harris, who had brutally murdered two young brothers years earlier in San Diego. While no one supported his unthinkable violence, and we wished only healing and peace for his victims' family, we did not want the killing to continue.

Many organized demonstrations, vigils, letter-writing campaigns, lobbying efforts, and prayer services to stop the murder of Robert Harris. What could I do? With other Jesuits, I was deeply involved in ongoing protests against U.S. military aid to El Salvador. We were still reeling from the massacre of six Jesuits and their coworkers a few months earlier. Yet a few miles away from the Berkeley hills on the San Francisco Bay, our government was planning with meticulous legal attention to murder someone at the San Quentin state prison.

I called the monsignor. "Do you think Mother Teresa would be willing to help us?"

"Of course she would want to help," he replied. "Here's her private phone number. I will be praying for all of you."

Nervous, anxious, filled with trepidation, I dialed the long number. Halfway around the world, thirteen and a half hours ahead of Berkeley, at 6:30 A.M., just after morning Mass, Mother Teresa picked up the phone in her office.

"Hello," she said in her heavy, unmistakable, Albanian-Indian accent.

I introduced myself, told her the situation, and asked if she would be willing to help us.

"What exactly did Robert Harris do?" she asked. I told her, then proposed that she speak with the California governor George Deukmejian by phone before the execution to ask for clemency.

"Yes, I will," she said, "and I will ask all the sisters at the Motherhouse here in Calcutta to pray for the governor." She spoke of her visit a few years earlier to San Quentin's death row. On the way out that day, she told a guard, "What you do to them, you do to God."

We made the arrangements. I called Governor Deukmejian's office and told them of Mother Teresa's call. On Monday evening, March 26, 1990, Mother Teresa spoke briefly with the governor. I called her back immediately after that to find out what happened, intending, as she agreed, to announce her message to the twenty reporters gathered in front of our Jesuit house.

"Did you speak with the governor?" I asked.

"Yes. He started talking about how he had to do this, that this was the law."

"What did you say?" I asked.

"I just said, 'Do what Jesus would do.' "

I was stunned. No arguments. No statistics. No invocation of sin or immorality or injustice. No lecture. No angry denunciation. Just: 'Do what Jesus would do."

"That's all I said. He talked again about how it was in the state's hand, so I repeated what I said, 'Do what Jesus would do if he was in your position.'

"We have to pray," she continued. "We all have to pray so that he receives the grace and the courage to do what Jesus would do. Pray hard. Get many people to pray for courage for him. Get everyone in the country to pray. And then, we have to respond to his decision with love and compassion. And keep praying for the family of the victims, too."

She asked me to call her again with any news and promised to help anytime.

Her message was simple and clear. Jesus was an opponent of the death penalty who himself was condemned to death, a prisoner on death row, legally executed by the authorities, a victim of the death penalty. It is all too clear what Jesus would do. He would not kill, no matter what the crime, no matter what the cause. He would grant clemency, demand forgiveness, and command nonviolent love.

The next morning, the *Los Angeles Times* carried a cartoon depicting Mother Teresa in one corner, speaking on the phone saying, "Do what Jesus would do if Jesus was in your position," and the governor in the other corner, on the phone asking, "What would Pilate do if Pilate was in my position?"

Miraculously, a California judge intervened a few days later and a stay was issued.

Two years passed. A new governor, Pete Wilson, who campaigned on a pledge to resume executions, set another date. Most Californians supported his "tough stand on crime." Despite eloquent opposition to the death penalty expressed by the Pope, bishops, and Mother Teresa, over 80 percent of all Catholics support executions. Most Christians and other people of faith do the same.

Mother Teresa repeated her message to Governor Wilson. "Do what Jesus would do."

But Wilson washed his hands of the case, and Harris was killed.

I called her with the news. After expressing her grief, she said, "God sees only love. God only sees the love that we put into what we do." She thanked all those who tried to save his life.

A year later, I received an urgent call that my friend Billy Neal Moore, a death row inmate in Georgia whom I had visited and corresponded with for years, was to be executed within days. Billy had been on death row longer than anyone else up to that time. He and a friend got drunk one night, robbed a liquor store, and killed its elderly owner. The next morning, he wept and begged forgiveness of his victim's family. He spent his years on death row praying, studying the scriptures, and counseling other inmates.

I flew to Georgia to be with Billy. We organized prayer services, press conferences, demonstrations, and vigils. Mother Teresa spoke on the phone to the chair of the Georgia Board of Pardon and Paroles, who had the authority to grant clemency before an execution. Mother Teresa promised that her community would keep a running prayer vigil. Meanwhile, Billy sent a message from prison, urging us to grant clemency in our hearts to all those who have personally hurt us. Otherwise, he said, we cannot expect God to take us seriously and answer our prayer for his clemency.

Several hours before the scheduled execution, the victim's family members appeared before the Board and pleaded for

Billy's life, saying that killing Billy would not bring their loved one back, nor end the killing, nor ease their pain.

In a historic decision, clemency was granted. Several months later, Billy was quietly released from prison. Today, he ministers to prisoners and teaches the Gospel of Jesus.

Not long afterward, I was ordained, then participated in an antinuclear demonstration. My friends and I hammered briefly on an F15-E nuclear-capable warplane, the kind used to drop bombs on Iraq during the Gulf War. Again I was trying to stop a killing. This time, it was the murder of our nation's hated enemies. Between 1993 and 1994, I spent eight long months in North Carolina jails. I received supportive letters from friends and family, but I was especially moved to receive words of encouragement from Billy and from Mother Teresa. "Be glad that you are to proclaim the love of Jesus even to the poor in prison," she wrote. "Give Jesus your pain and limitation and trust in Him. In your weakness His power will be a protection and a strength."

In 1995, in Rome, I met Mother Teresa at her order's headquarters. She was severely stooped by then. When we were introduced, she reached up and put her hands firmly on my cheeks and held them there for about fifteen seconds, while she smiled and stared into my eyes. Then, she folded her arms, with a stern look, as if to reprimand me for doubting her. She asked with a suppressed chuckle, "What did I say they should do?"

"You said they should do what Jesus would do," I answered.

"And what did they do for your friend?"

"They did what Jesus would do; they granted him clemency."

"Thank God!" she said with an enormous smile. She was filled with joy at Billy's clemency. She asked about him, and about my own work, and promised that her sisters would pray for me for the rest of my life.

That day in Rome, I experienced a tremendous love pouring from Mother Teresa. If love is all God sees, as she told me, then I'm sure that God saw her that day. Her entire being radiated unconditional love.

Though Mother Teresa was famous for her compassion for the poor and her advocacy for the unborn, she was equally strong in her opposition to the death penalty and to war. How could she do otherwise, since she sought so passionately to practice the love of Jesus?

When I think of her now, I remember her voice, and her simple, stunning wisdom: *Do what Jesus would do*. With these five words, Mother Teresa offers us all a mantra, a practical solution, a way out of the world's violence. She calls each of us—from governors and presidents to parents and church-goers—to live out the love of God, not only to show compassion to the poor and needy, but to speak out against executions, bombing raids, and the nuclear threat. She wants us not only to read about Jesus and to think about Jesus, but to do what Jesus did.

Simple advice, yes, but rarely put so bluntly in the face of a politically charged issue. As we do what we can to abolish the death penalty; as we try in our own way to do what Jesus would do if he were in our shoes; as we too radiate unconditional, compassionate love; God will see each one of us and will grant the same verdict: clemency for all, a life of peace.

15

Resisting Evil

In 1985, I flew alone to El Salvador to spend the summer working with Jesuits as they set up a refugee camp in the countryside. El Salvador was in the midst of a ferocious civil war, which had left over 75,000 people dead by the end of the 1980s. A far-right-wing government, sponsored and funded by the United States, armed death squads that roamed the country killing anyone who spoke out for freedom or social justice. Nearly all of El Salvador's five million people live in abject poverty. The loudest voices for justice and peace came from the churches. Eighteen priests, several nuns, and hundreds of catechists were assassinated. Archbishop Oscar Romero was assassinated while celebrating Mass on March 24, 1980. As I walked through the Salvador airport that hot spring morning, I thought first of the four American churchwomen, who were last seen arriving there before they were kidnapped, raped, and killed, on December 2, 1980. Machine gun–carrying soldiers casually strolled through the airport while military jeeps filled the road to San Salvador.

If ever there was a country that cried out for justice and nonviolence, it is El Salvador.

When I arrived, the Jesuits of El Salvador were already legendary around the world for their outspoken stand for justice and peace. After Jesuit Father Rutilio Grande was assassinated on March 12, 1977, his friend Oscar Romero dramatically changed from a quiet, conservative cleric to a thunderous prophet who shook the nation and the world with his urgent call for justice for the poor and an end to greed and violence. Other Jesuits stood by him, offering advice, writing pastoral letters, and helping as needed.

After Romero's death, Salvadoran Jesuits wrote two public letters to Jesuits in North America, calling on us to do whatever we could to stop billions of dollars in U.S. weapons and military aid from flowing to El Salvador, so that the killing would cease. My friends and I prayed over those letters, joined demonstrations against U.S. militarism in Central America, walked in solidarity with Salvadoran refugees, studied Spanish, organized teach-ins, and lobbied members of Congress, trying our best to answer our brothers' urgent call.

I felt called to travel to Central America and witness for myself the struggle for life and justice there. I wanted to meet those heroic Jesuits. I spent that summer helping the Archdiocese of San Salvador establish a refugee camp near Guasapa, a volcano that was being bombed daily by U.S. warplanes to terrorize not only the rebels but the local *campesinos* (impoverished farmers who make up 90 percent of the population) who supported them. I spent several months clearing fields, planting corn, entertaining children, and listening to the stories of the suffering refugees.

During my first week, I visited the Jesuits at their university in San Salvador. At the center of their extraordinary work stood the university president, the Jesuit philosopher and theologian Ignacio Ellacuria. Several other young Jesuits and I had scheduled an afternoon meeting with him to hear his reflections on his work and on El Salvador. He began: "The purpose of the Jesuit University here in El Salvador is to promote the reign of God."

I was dumbfounded. I could not imagine the president of Georgetown or Marquette or Fordham ever saying outright that the purpose of a Jesuit university in the United States is to promote the reign of God! Such grandiose talk is rarely heard in the halls of U.S. Catholic academic institutions.

"To promote the reign of God is to work for peace and justice," Ellacuria continued. "But you can no longer claim to stand for God's reign of peace and justice unless you also stand up publicly against the antireign of war and injustice!"

Here in a nutshell was the struggle in El Salvador, in Latin America, the essence of the Church, and the vocation of the disciple of Jesus in our tumultuous times.

In our world of war, starvation, and violence, you can no longer just try to do good. You also have to resist evil. If you do not publicly resist evil, your goodness merely quietly props up the structures of evil, which destroy the lives of the poor and marginalized. The times have forced us, whether we like it or not, to resist evil as well as to do good.

Gandhi put it this way: "Noncooperation with evil is as much a duty as cooperation with good."

Ellacuria's words hit me hard. That evening, I saw for myself how he lived out that profound mission. The Jesuit university community threw a party to welcome us. We sat around a big table, drank beer, and ate rice and beans late into the night, listening to our elders' stories. Their house was located on the corner in a middle-class neighborhood, two blocks from the university. The dining room table sat before the front window. As we ate, they pointed out the bullet holes around the room, even on the chairs. They had been bombed twenty-one times since the late 1970s, endured several drive-by shootings, and received countless death threats.

"Tell them about the time the bomb went off outside your window," Ellacuria said with a smile at one of the others. The bomb went off about 4 A.M., blew out the window, and threw the bed across the room, but the Jesuit remained asleep! We all burst out laughing, despite the terror of the act.

The cost of speaking truth, denouncing injustice, announcing justice, doing good, and resisting evil stood before me. These men risked their lives just as Martin Luther King, Jr., Mahatma Gandhi, Oscar Romero, and Jesus. Yet they exuded contentment, determination, faith in God, even joy.

When six of these Jesuits were ordered out of their home, forced to lie on the ground, and shot point blank in the early morning hours of November 16, 1989, they paid the ultimate price for their lifelong nonviolent resistance to evil. They suffered and died, like the One they followed. And like Christ, they rose to new life, inspiring people throughout North America to demand an end to the war in El Salvador. Their martyrdom changed El Salvador, and made peace possible. As my friends and I prayed, fasted, spoke, and demonstrated for an end to U.S. military aid to El Salvador, we knew that one day, evil would be overcome by good.

As Dr. King used to say over and over again, quoting William Cullen Bryant, "Truth crushed to earth will rise again."

"Christians and all those who hate injustice are obligated to fight it with every ounce of their strength," Ignacio Ellacuria wrote. "They must work for a new world in which greed and selfishness will finally be overcome."

As the war finally ended in El Salvador, many of us turned our attention to the School of the Americas (SOA) in Fort Benning, Georgia, where the U.S. trains thousands of Latin American soldiers to kill. Nineteen of the twenty-six soldiers convicted in the murder of the Jesuits were trained at this "School of Assassins." In its fifty-year history, the SOA has quietly readied over 60,000 troops. The Latin American nations with the worst human rights records have consistently sent the most soldiers to the SOA.

In the early 1990s, Roy Bourgeois, a Maryknoll priest who had spent many years working among victims of war in Central America, began a permanent peace vigil outside its gate and started the "SOA Watch," a campaign to close the School of the Americas. Over the years, hundreds have gathered on the anniversary of the Jesuit massacre to pray, hold vigils and "cross the line" onto the base in an act of nonviolent civil disobedience, calling for the school's closing. Dozens of people—priests, nuns, students, and grandmothers—have spent months to years in prison for their peaceful resistance, and they keep coming back.

In November 1990, a dozen people gathered for prayer at

the entrance to the base. By November 1998, over 7,000 people of faith and conscience from nearly every state came together to pray and protest at Fort Benning. Saturday brought an all-day vigil at the entrance to the SOA, with music and speakers, guests from Central America, and nonviolent civil disobedience training. I had the opportunity to speak, to describe my visits in 1985 with the six Jesuits who were later so brutally massacred by SOA graduates. I repeated what Ellacuria had said to me.

On Sunday, after prayers, a memorial dance by a Guatemalan family, and a reading of our covenant of nonviolence, we lined up four abreast in a solemn funeral procession, carrying coffins symbolizing the SOA's victims, and walked silently onto the base.

We had hoped perhaps a thousand people would cross the line. But the spirit among us was strong that morning and, at final count, 2,370 people risked arrest by walking onto the base. It was one of the largest acts of nonviolent civil disobedience in decades.

When we reached the wall of police and soldiers, actor Martin Sheen knelt down and began to pray. He was immediately hauled away. The authorities quickly filled twenty-five buses, but they only held half the group. The police and base authorities were caught off guard by the massive, peaceful crowds. Instead of processing us, they drove 1,300 of us two miles to a park and released us. Hours later, they dropped off the second batch of 1,000 protesters.

After walking back through the neighborhoods to the SOA entrance, Martin Sheen introduced the youngest protester: Bernadette O'Neill, age ten, who said that the killing promoted by the SOA is wrong, and the time has come to stop it.

One year later, in November 1999, on the tenth anniversary of the Jesuit massacre, over twelve thousand people turned up to speak out against the SOA and to demand its closing. A historic vote in the U.S. Congress earlier that summer particularly cut funding to the school, at a time when military spending was increased by billions of dollars. This time, 4,408 of us crossed the line. And we will keep coming back until the entire "School of Assassins" is closed.

This amazing effort to stop evil epitomizes the work of the peacemaker. As long as injustice and violence exist, they must be resisted. As long as there is resistance in a spirit of prayerful nonviolence, we can trust that a new day of peace with justice will one day dawn.

16.

Standing with the Poor

How we view the world depends on where we stand. If we stand with the wealthy, we will contemplate the world from the heights of privilege and domination. If, however, we stand with those who are poor and marginalized, oppressed and persecuted, then we shall contemplate the world from the experience of suffering and injustice. From this bottom-up perspective, we have a better chance of glimpsing the world as God does.

When we stand in solidarity with black South Africans who resisted apartheid, death row inmates pleading for clemency, starving children in the slums of Cité Soleil, Haiti, and homeless people on the bitter streets of Washington, D.C., we can know the realities of systemic violence. As we turn to God from within this poverty and oppression, we meet not a false god of domination who blesses oppression, not a false god of injustice, racism, and classism, but the living God who liberates us all and calls us to live as equal sisters and brothers, all God's children.

Jesus spent his public life serving those in need in the province of Palestine on the outskirts of the Roman Empire. From his life on the edge, his life among the poor, he spoke of a God of justice and mercy. He severely criticized injustice and those who perpetrated it. At one point, he clearly decided to walk to the center of religious life, the Temple in Jerusalem, where he overturned the tables of the moneychangers, and directly challenged the systematic oppression of the poor carried out in the name of God. The Temple system blessed the Empire's economic oppression of the poor. It said that true worship of God required a large financial payment for a sacrificial dove or pigeon, so that one's prayer would be pure and acceptable. In the process, the Temple acted as a national bank, offering loans, keeping track of debts, and changing money for payment of the Temple tax. In Jesus' mind, the culture had desecrated this sacred place "from a house of prayer into a robber's den."

As a contemplative, Jesus was repulsed by this institutionalized injustice, all done in God's name. He took action for justice, turning over the tables of the moneychangers and the seats of the dove sellers, refusing to permit any one to carry anything through the Temple, and calling for a true "house of prayer." By his example, Jesus taught that we cannot be peace-making contemplatives if we silently allow injustice to flourish around us. He stood with the poor all his life, and in the end, his solidarity with the poor cost him his life. Jesus let their pain and suffering touch him, so that he not only showed compassion and love for them but stood up to defend them. He never hurt or kill anyone, but Jesus was deliberately active on behalf of the poor, and definitely nonviolent. (According to John's Gospel he took a type of cord that was used solely to round up cattle and drove out the animals from the Temple.) His action is provocative, dangerous, civilly disobedient, and illegal. Within days, perhaps hours, he was arrested, jailed, tried, tortured, and executed. Through it all, he expected his followers to also stand with the poor and undertake similar actions for justice for the poor.

We, too, must stand among the poor and disenfranchised. We must walk in solidarity with those who suffer, accompany them, be present with them, listen to them, learn from them, and ultimately resist injustice, and suffer and die with them. In the world of the poor, we are offered new eyes to see reality. As we walk with them, we see God present among them. With the eyes of faith and love, we see that God is here among us in the homeless, the sick, the tortured, the imprisoned, the condemned, the naked, the thirsty, the hungry, and the dying. There, where we least expect to find God, we see God. As we discover God in the face of the poor, we will be moved in a spirit of love and truth to act for justice and peace on their behalf.

St. Francis understood the importance of living life in this way. A man of prayer, he experienced a conversion when he gave his coat to a leper and kissed him. From that moment on, he wanted to serve Christ in the poor, and in this way, to become an instrument of God's peace. More than anyone, he understood the connection between voluntary poverty and active nonviolence.

In our own time, Dorothy Day lived in Catholic Worker communities with the homeless she sheltered for nearly fifty years. This life she chose moved her closer to God. Each morning before attending Mass at the local parish, she spent two hours praying the Psalms and meditating on the Gospel. From this contemplative grounding, she lived her life of voluntary poverty and hospitality, and spoke out for justice and peace. The interaction between solidarity and contemplation became the core of her life. This life of prayer among the poor led her to call for an end to the war-making system that robs the poor of the funds they need for basic human needs, and to point to the peace that comes from serving one another and worshiping the God of peace and justice.

Similarly, Gandhi also spent long hours each day in silent prayer, as he struggled to live among the poor "as one of them."

"Recall the face of the poorest and most helpless person you have ever seen," Gandhi advised, "and ask yourself if the next step you contemplate is going to be of any use to him [or her]." Gandhi knew that the road to peace was a prayerful journey in solidarity with the poor and marginalized.

There is nothing romantic about working with and serving unemployed, low-income, and marginalized peoples. They are as demanding as anyone else. They are human like the rest of us, except they have fewer resources, greater barriers to overcome, and enormous hardships. But because they have so few earthly possessions, so little power or control, they more often turn to God for help. This bottom line dependency ironically encourages a basic faith and hope that escapes the rest of us. "Blessed are the poor," Jesus says in the Beatitudes. "Theirs is the reign of God." Though the poor may not have the luxuries and opportunities the rest of us privileged people have, they have one possession we do not have: a full share in the reign of God. This is one of the mysteries of life. The challenge for us is to walk among the poor, to become downwardly mobile, and so one day to share their life and with them, God's reign of peace.

One of the best models I ever knew of dedicated solidarity with the world's poor was Mev Puleo, a thirty-four-year-old photojournalist. When she was fourteen, her family took her on a trip to Rio de Janeiro, where she rode the tour bus up the mountain to see the famous stone-carved statue of Christ the Redeemer with his open, outstretched arms. As the bus climbed the mountain, she saw on one side the luxurious hotels and tourist shops, and on the other side, the desperate dilapidated shacks, ragged children, and starving adults. She was terribly upset by the poverty she witnessed, and decided to try to do what she could to fight poverty and relieve the sufferings of the poor.

Eventually she became a photographer who profiled the faces of people living in poverty. Her mission in life was to befriend the suffering, to stand with them, to show their face to the world, and to proclaim their right to life. She traveled frequently throughout Latin America, from Brazil to Haiti, learning how to advocate for the poor, but also worked among the homeless in St. Louis, Boston and Oakland. Over time, she came to see discipleship to Christ as a life of solidarity with the poor. Through her daily meditations, she stayed centered in Christ's peace and grew ever more committed to Christ present in the suffering people of the world.

Then without any warning, on Easter Sunday, 1993, she developed a speech impediment. Doctors informed her that she had a massive brain tumor. Despite a ten-hour operation to remove the tumor and months of chemotherapy and radiation, she would live only about a year. Toward the end of her life she became paralyzed and lost her sight, and her last few weeks were a living agony. But she died peacefully on January 12, 1996, with her family around her. All her life she had identified and suffered with people in pain. In her suffering and death, her solidarity became complete.

"Yes, the way up the hill to Christ the Redeemer is a bumpy, sometimes dangerous ride," she wrote shortly before her death. "I have come to believe that we the privileged are invited to get off the bus and plant our feet squarely beside the journeying people, walking with the God, who is present along the road. We may all start at different places, but we will arrive together as we learn to walk with one another."

Mev Puleo modeled the contemplative life because her life of prayer was rooted in her direct experience among the poor and suffering. She encountered Christ in the world's poor. When she, too, suffered and died, she was able to accept her death in peace, giving thanks for her lifelong journey among Christ in the poor. Because of the great love she shared with many people, her deep desire to touch others with the love she experienced among the poor, and her passionate concern for the truth of justice and peace, her life and death affected thousands across the hemisphere. She lived the life of peace.

From 1995 to 1996, I worked in the impoverished south-side section of Richmond, Virginia, directing the Sacred Heart Center, a community center for low-income, African American women and children, created from an abandoned former parochial school. With over thirty people on staff (a third of them women from the neighborhood), the Sacred Heart Center offers a large variety of programs to meet the needs of neighborhood families, including day care, after-school and summer programs, and a family literacy program.

The Sacred Heart Center opens at six-thirty each morning when the day-care children arrive. By eight-thirty women and children in the family literacy program arrive. These women spend their mornings studying and sharing time with their children, to strengthen bonds and improve parenting skills. Classes run through the day. At 3 P.M. buses pick up about a hundred kids, ages five to eighteen, who attend the center's after school program, which offers tutoring, snacks, sports, and other activities. The center also hosts an array of boys and girls clubs, and early childhood classes, and each day, bustles with meals, youth groups, basketball games, aerobics, talks, health classes, and videos. All programs are provided free or for only a nominal donation.

In the center's neighborhood, 77 percent of residents over twenty-five have less than a high school education, 60 percent earn below the poverty level, 65 percent of households are single-parent, and 40 percent of all residents are school-age children. Every day I witnessed a constant struggle to find hope in the midst of despair, love in a world of indifference, community in the midst of fear, nonviolence in the midst of violence, life in the midst of death. During my tenure Richmond had the second-highest murder rate in the country. During one week, thirteen people were shot in our neighborhood alone.

In this context of poverty and violence, the mission of the Sacred Heart Center is simple: "to be a sign of hope and strength for the vulnerable individuals and families of our neighborhood." But this is an enormous undertaking. By working with kids and their moms, the center seeks to accompany the neighborhood families, address the roots of neighborhood violence and poverty, strengthen the lives of the struggling people, and reverse the deadly trends among young people.

Every day there was a revelation about the day-to-day life and death in which the poor engage. I vividly remember one evening driving a van of mothers and their children from the center through the neighborhood to their homes. They had just attended their weekly parents' counseling meeting, where they learn nonviolent ways of child-raising. On the way, the women spoke casually about recent local murders. "Did you know the thirteen-year-old girl found dead on Saturday morning in the crack house?" one woman asked. "The people at the morgue called me today to ask if I would come down and identify a body they thought might be my sister-in-law," another woman said. Violence and death are the standard topics of conversation there because they have become routine.

I asked the women how their meeting went and what they

thought of the Sacred Heart Center. They all smiled. They said the center gives them the strength and the support, not only in raising their kids, but to carry on. "It gives me hope for the future of my family," one mom said. "I just feel hope." As I looked into their faces, I, too, felt renewed hope.

By walking with my beautiful neighbors in the midst of brutal poverty, I saw the world with new eyes. Because I saw injustice every day, and listened to it constantly, I saw the world just a bit more as God sees it—in all its pain and sorrow, injustice and oppression, racism and sexism, classism and privilege, violence and death. Away from this day-to-day reality check, I can easily forget others' suffering and return to my own comforts. The day-to-day experience of the unjust sufferings of the poor broke my heart. It also entered and shaped my contemplative life. As I tried to accompany Jesus and stay centered in the God of peace, my inner life was filled with concern for my suffering, struggling friends. But that pain brought out new compassion, greater love, a deeper faith, and a stronger inner peace, despite the surrounding turmoil.

Life among the poor is not easy. Their suffering and injustice is very real and shocking and deadly. But my struggling friends teach me to surrender ever more fully to God, to trust completely in God, to put God and the needs of others first. In other words, I find myself becoming more human. The disenfranchised people I have known and loved help me to see what is most important in life, to live solely in the spirit of God, as they do, and to be as loving and compassionate as I can be. By standing with the poor, I have discovered, they stand with us and teach us and disarm us and in the end, share with us the peace of God which God has given them.

If we stand with the poor, walk with them, and share their life, then they will share with us the one thing they have, a taste of life in the reign of God. Though my own experiences among the suffering and marginalized have been gut-wrenching and heartbreaking, I have felt deeply blessed. Through their loving kindness, I've been granted a glimpse of God's reign of peace.

Solidarity with the poor then not only keeps us grounded in the reality of poverty, injustice, and oppression; it not only helps us grow in compassion and love; it not only deepens awareness about our human dependence on God; it leads us to peace.

17.

Witnessing for Peace

If we want to be voices for peace, sometimes we have to take a public stand and offer ourselves as witnesses. My life has become one long experiment in witness—from daily conversations with those who support the latest war to speaking out in prayer services and press conferences. Once in a while, I even undertake some bold act, trying to emulate the daring spirit of the Acts of the Apostles.

Once that meant paddling a canoe down a river to protest the launching of a Trident nuclear submarine. Like those early apostles, instead of receiving acceptance or applause, I was accused of drinking too early in the morning and arrested.

How does one witness against a Trident nuclear submarine?

First, you and your friends should find an unobtrusive, secluded spot to lower your canoe into the river (in this case, the

Thames River in Connecticut). Mind you, a few hundred yards
down river at the Electric Boat nuclear submarine plant in
Groton, Connecticut, police and security guards are on the
lookout for anyone who might disrupt the festivities.

On the day of my witness, they were launching the fif-
teenth Trident submarine, the U.S.S. *Rhode Island*, the deadliest
weapon ever created in the history of the world.

You have to take care not to attract attention. Despite our
best efforts, a local woman spotted me and my friends and immediately alerted the police about our suspicious activities
with a canoe. But before the police boat could pull ashore, my
companions and I pulled ourselves out, and began walking as
unobtrusively as possible down a sidestreet with the canoe in
hand, looking a little too much like the Three Stooges.

Five blocks down, we found a secluded spot between two
houses where we set the canoe back in the water. Wearing life
vests and armed only with one huge banner—TRIDENT IS A
CRIME; SWORDS INTO PLOWSHARES—and a roofing hammer (in
case, by the grace of God, we were able to reach the sub itself
and begin to nonviolently dismantle it), we took off down the
river.

The sky overhead shone a clear, bright blue. A cool breeze
was blowing and the Thames River sparkled. Across the river
we could see the military town of New London, Connecticut.
Two hundred and two dual capable (nuclear/conventional)

submarines have been built in Groton over the last few decades. Police and Coast Guard cruise the river to ensure the launching ceremonies, attended by thousands of military and guests, proceed undisturbed. Two friends paddled, while another friend and I attempted to unfurl the banner at just the right moment.

Meanwhile, seventeen other peacemaking friends were entering Electric Boat to attend the public ceremonies. They entered in pairs and walked down the narrow entranceway, where they knelt down and spoke out against the Trident, obstructing the crowds from entering. After five minutes, one pair was arrested and escorted to a waiting van, but they were followed by another pair who knelt down to call a halt to the proceedings. And on it went.

The current was fast and we were clipping along the river. Disregarding the police boats that were now flashing their lights and heading straight for us, we were concerned about the choppy waves, especially the large wakes from other boats that whizzed by. We didn't want to capsize. Our goal was to paddle to the crowded Trident dock and try to climb onto the dock to witness for peace. The sun was hot and we could hear a military band. In just minutes, with the help of a strong current, we were one hundred yards in front of the Trident dock. The absurdity of the situation then hit me full force.

Not the absurdity of paddling a canoe down the Thames

River to the Trident dock. Not the absurdity of friends blockading the entrance to a military ceremony. No, the full-scale, monstrous absurdity, the total lunacy of the Trident submarine itself.

There it stood. Right before us, decorated with flags. The U.S.S. *Rhode Island* was lowered almost to the water in a special dock, covered with white tents for the celebration. Right beside it, completely out of the water, aimed straight at us like a giant, terrorist bomb was the U.S.S. *Maine*, set to be launched months later.

Lunacy, indeed. Why do we need such weapons? What has happened to us as a people that we continue to build them? What must God think as we celebrate these instruments of death? Such thoughts ran through my mind as I shook my head in disbelief.

But seeing is believing. There on the shoreline were two submarines—each the equivalent of four thousand Hiroshima bombs; each designed for first-strike nuclear attack; each built at the cost of $2.2 billion. Think about what $2.2 billion could otherwise buy: housing for the homeless, food for the malnourished and the starving, healthcare, jobs, education, AIDS research, and environmental cleanup. The Cold War is long over. The Soviet Union has withered away. But still we build, we maintain, we launch new Trident submarines. The Trident in its very existence violates God's commandments "Thou

141

Shalt Not Kill" and "Love Your Enemies." It also violates international law, prohibiting the construction and use of weapons of mass destruction. Yet here they are. And we continue to build more—to reach a fleet of nineteen Trident submarines.

A Coast Guard ship approached us. "Fellows, there are too many of you in that small canoe, so we're going to have to escort you back to shore."

"No, sir, officer," I replied with a smile. "We're fine."

"Come on, we know who you are and what you're about," he announced, as his boat rubbed against our flimsy canoe and we held on, trying not to capsize. "We're escorting you back now."

But the police and Coast Guard ships inadvertently brought us closer to the Trident dock.

Ever compliant, we obeyed. Then, as we passed in front of the Trident, we turned and paddled right toward the ceremony. We unfurled the banner. On the dock a crowd gathered to watch the spectacle. The police boat was suddenly on top of us again and a voice declared, "Okay, fellas, that's enough. You're going to have to come with us." But the closeness of the boat and canoe and the choppy waters threw our balance. One friend jumped in the water, the canoe started to sink, and the next thing I knew, I was swimming!

"Swim to the back of the boat and we'll pull you on

board," one officer said. I turned and saw the Trident. In a flash, all those swimming lessons from summer camp returned and I was off. I headed straight for the Trident. Two other friends were swimming, too. The police boats circled around.

The water, though polluted, was cool and refreshing. As we swam, we stopped occasionally to speak out in a loud voice, not only to the dumbfounded Coast Guard crews in the distance but to the crowds of military officers, Electric Boat workers, and guests standing along the dock next to the Trident. "I am a Jesuit, a Catholic priest, and I work with the homeless and the poor. The Trident is a sin, a crime against God and humanity. It robs the poor of the world. The billions spent on this submarine should be spent on housing, food, healthcare, and education. The Trident is not something to celebrate. It is Auschwitz. It threatens to destroy the planet. For God's sake, please dismantle it. Learn the way of peace and nonviolence."

Suddenly, a specially equipped rubber police raft sped across the river and fished me out of the water. "Officers, we mean you no harm," I said. "It's just that we have to speak out against this death machine."

"We understand," they replied. "We respect you, but we have to take you in."

Soaking wet, I arrived with my friends at the Groton City Jail. We were photographed, questioned, processed and escorted into a crowded jail cell, where we found the seventeen others waiting, and they drowned us with applause. As we settled down for a day in jail, the group exploded into song:

Paul and Silas bound in jail, had no money to pay their bail.
Keep your eyes on the prize. Hold on.
The only thing that we did wrong was stay in the wilderness too long.
Keep your eyes on the prize. Hold on.
The only thing that we did right was to organize for life.
Keep your eyes on the prize. Hold on.
The only Trident we can stand is the sugarless chewing brand.
Keep your eyes on the prize. Hold on.

Eventually, we were released and instructed to appear in court a few weeks later. A police officer smiled at me and said, "You know, we respect and admire you for staying at this for so long, but you should know, we think you're crazy." I returned the smile and offered a blessing.

It wasn't the first time I've been called crazy. I thought of St. Paul, encouraging me to be a fool for Christ. In a world that constructs and launches Trident submarines, what harm is there in being mocked for speaking out for peace? I left the jail smiling.

We can't all swim out in front of Trident submarines, but we can all do something to witness for peace. Whatever challenges face us, each one of us can voice our hope for peace and justice, for a world without Trident submarines and weapons of mass destruction. Whatever the tactic or action we take, we can do it with a good heart and a loving disposition, knowing that the God of peace will take care of the outcome. As more and more of us clamor for peace, God's plan for a disarmed world will one day come true.

18.

Disarming the World

The most daring disarmament action I ever undertook landed me in jail for eight months. On December 7, 1993, Pearl Harbor Day, three friends and I walked onto the Seymour Johnson Air Force Base in Goldsboro, North Carolina, in the middle of full-scale war games. We hammered on an F15-E nuclear-capable fighter-bomber, enacting the prophet Isaiah's vision to "beat swords into plowshares" and "study war no more."

It was at once the most terrifying and most grace-filled experience of my life.

We expected to walk through the woods and fields to the tarmac without seeing anyone, but we found ourselves in the middle of thousands of soldiers preparing for war, willing to unleash a firestorm of destruction on other human beings, if necessary, even nuclear weapons. I was so scared. We had not only trespassed on government property, we had passed large signs that read, SOLDIERS ARE UNDER ORDERS TO SHOOT AND KILL ANY TRESPASSERS ON SIGHT.

As I read those signs and thought of the risks we faced, I also thought of the many people I had known who had died from war in El Salvador. I thought of the millions—billions?—who have died from war throughout history. I recalled the great saints and peacemakers who risked their lives for peace. And I thought of Jesus, who died telling us to "put away the sword" and "love your enemies." With every step, I took a deep breath and prayed that God would be with us and bless us and give me the strength to do God's will.

In an act of faith, filled with the presence of the God of peace, we decided to keep walking forward. When we eventually reached the tarmac, we found one fighter-bomber that had no soldiers around it, and started hammering on it. I hammered twice, not even putting a dent or chipping the paint of the aircraft, but praying all the time for an end to war and the abolition of all nuclear weapons and weapons of mass destruction.

Within seconds, we were immediately surrounded by soldiers carrying machine guns. "We are unarmed, nonviolent people," I said on our behalf. "We mean you no harm. We're just here to dismantle this weapon of death."

This was not well received.

For a moment, the soldiers stared at us in disbelief with their guns continually aimed. Since they were in the midst of war games, they were caught off guard. Then one of them started shouting, "This is the real world! This is the real world!" to convince the others that the games were over, that we had disrupted their activity. Another yelled at us, "You can't do that! Put your hands up! Face down on the ground!" We were searched, pushed around, and arrested. With our faces in the ground, we joined hands, thanked God for the action, and prayed the Lord's Prayer. Then we were handcuffed and driven to separate holding areas. Hours later, we were taken to jail, arraigned, and charged with two felony counts: destruction of government property and conspiracy to commit a felony.

With the blow of a hammer, my life was changed forever. I faced twenty years in prison, and I learned the bitter reality of life behind bars. I also learned new spiritual, biblical lessons about the struggle for peace, the paschal mystery, and the potentially explosive depths of nonviolence.

Talk about disturbing the peace! We had disrupted Air Force war games. We had walked through the "Shoot to Kill" zone in our trespassing. We had symbolically damaged nuclear fighter-bombers. But we had also disturbed the peace of our own lives, friendships, family relationships, jobs, and future plans. By risking disarmament, we risked our own lives. Everything was now up for grabs.

I'll never forget watching as one officer started yelling directly into the face of my friend Philip Berrigan, the longtime peace activist and brother of Daniel Berrigan, saying, "Did you put a bomb in that plane?" Phil looked back quizzically, and asked, "What do you think we are, crazy?"

At one point around four o'clock in the morning, as we walked through the massive base, we rested on a bluff overlooking the tarmac and saw the entire base spread out in front of us, like three airports with thousands of military personnel milling about. With a shock we saw with our own eyes the scary picture of reality: While the nation sleeps, the war machine barrels on in the middle of the night, full steam ahead, preparing for the next great war. The seventy-five F15-E fighters on the tarmac were on alert to bomb Bosnia. In fact, the F15-E was the weapon of choice throughout the Gulf War. It was used on Ash Wednesday, February 12, 1991, to drop two smart bombs on the Ameriyah shelter, killing over 1,200 women and children in Baghdad. Toward the end of that war, it was used to kill tens of thousands of Iraqis fleeing from Kuwait to Basra on what came to be known as the "highway of death." Each fighter can also carry nuclear weapons. At the time, they were the cutting edge of U.S. military technology, the force of destruction itself. If we are to ever fully worship the God of peace and learn to live in peace, one day all of these weapons will have to be disarmed.

The world is brimming with such weapons. Over 5,000 nuclear weapons remain poised today on hair-trigger alert, ready to fire at a minute's notice. Over 36,000 nuclear warheads fill arsenals around the world, with combined explosive yield of 650,000 Hiroshima bombs. (Over thirty U.S. nuclear weapons have been involved in accidents.) Meanwhile, the trillions of dollars spent on preparations for mass destruction mean trillions of dollars taken from starving children, the homeless, better schools, jobs, cleaning up the environment, and healthcare for all.

Over 130 million people died from war during the last century. Yet we still refuse to accept its futility. Civilians, mainly children and the elderly, die needlessly by the hundreds of thousands each year. Hundreds of thousands of people continued to be maimed by land mines, long after the wars are over. Radiation and other destructive war chemicals poison the land and water, deforming newborn children and killing thousands for years to come. And still, we wage war.

If we are going to end war, dismantle our weapons, learn to live together nonviolently, we are going to have to change the direction of the world. We are going to have to renounce the intent to wage war and create a nonmilitary society. Such change will cost everything—everything except our lives and the lives of generations to come. Every one of us will have to participate in this social-political-economic conversion.

For me, the cost of disarmament came in the long hard months we spent in jail after our action. For eight and a half months, from December 7, 1993, until July 22, 1994, I sat in a tiny cell in the Edenton County Jail with my friends Philip Berrigan and Bruce Friedrich, contemplating our disarmament action and the God of peace who called us to enact it. During our long days in jail, we never went outdoors, never had a walk, and never had any privacy. Our cell contained an open steel toilet and cold metal bunk beds. The cell next to ours was identical. The connecting room between our cells had a TV and a narrow metal table that lined a narrow wall. The food trays were shoved at us through a slot in the door. Our fourth group member, Lynn Fredriksson, sat in the crowded women's cell in the Elizabeth City Jail.

Though Thoreau, Gandhi, Dr. King, Dorothy Day, and others have advocated civil disobedience and imprisonment as the way to social change, there is nothing romantic about jail. Prison is a terrible, terrifying experience. Today, over two million people suffer in jails and prisons, and the numbers will rise as we continue to build new prisons instead of schools, homes, and employment opportunities.

The whole prison system is meant to oppress people, and it does just that. There is no way it can "rehabilitate" people or make them whole again. I do not have the words to describe what it is like to be locked in a tiny room for so long, to be treated so inhumanly, to be faced with such state-sanctioned violence. There is no way that this current system will ever make people nonviolent. We found ourselves struggling to maintain our patience and nonviolence, even after a lifetime of trying to be nonviolent. Our fellow prisoners did not have our training or background, and quickly succumbed to provocation, anger, despair, hate, and violence. This was only natural since we were all treated as animals, not human beings.

I remember one night early on in one of the first jails we were in, when our group was separated and I was feeling all alone in a crowded cell with eight other angry prisoners wearing orange jumpsuits, when a fight broke out in the cell next to ours, and somehow, they managed to steal a broom and nearly kill one another. One person was taken away unconscious, and the floor was covered in blood. I was terrified, and turned to the Psalms, where I discovered many prayers from prison to the God of prisoners. Slowly, regularly, hourly, through prayer and scripture, I was able to move from terror to trust, from darkness to light, from fear to faith.

In the Edenton County Jail, where we were locked in our tiny cell for seven months, the claustrophobia began to eat away at me. The monotony and confinement made time stand still. There were moments of deep depression. Though I was supported by many people, still many other friends and family members denounced me and my action, and such rejection was hard to take, especially sitting all alone on my jail bunk bed. Each day, each hour, indeed, every ten minutes or so, I struggled to reject despair and cling to hope and to the God of peace. I kept reminding myself to reject the hate and indifference of the world, to choose again the transforming spirit of love for humanity that pushed me to undertake our action in the first place.

In the midst of this deprivation and degradation, we were granted a rare kind of peace. Though our action upset many people and often seemed to bear no positive result, its spiritual roots grew and bore fruit in a deep sense of personal meaning and spiritual purpose. Each day I sat on my bunk bed to center myself in the moment. Through mindfulness and prayer, I survived the daily drudgery, and could even enter the beauty of the present moment. Never before have I felt so claustrophobic, and yet never before have I been so centered in God.

My friends and I spent hours every day studying the scriptures, sharing Eucharist, writing letters, and talking with one another and with other inmates. We shared our lives, our hopes, our pain, and our faith. But there was no place to go. We sat there in peace, as best we could. Throughout the day I would try to return to that quiet center. In that stillness, helplessness, powerlessness, we surrendered our hearts to God and our lives to God's own peace.

During that time, my spirit was sorely tested. I was con-

fronted by everything—my many limitations and powerlessness, my inner violence and desire for nonviolence, faith and
faithlessness, hope and despair, sorrow and joy, loneliness and
community. (I recorded the whole experience in a diary that
was later published as a book entitled, *Peace Behind Bars: A
Journal from Jail.*) With the help of my friends, I endured the
ordeal. And my conviction and hope for disarmament deepened. I believed even more that we were right to hammer on
those fighter planes; that the God of peace calls the nations of
the world to disarm now and renounce war forever; that in fact
more and more people will have to engage in such nonviolent
civil disobedience if we are going to have a future of peace.

Our government will never dismantle its nuclear arsenal
unless ordinary people of faith like us demand it. The government can only promise future bloodshed and the death of millions with its weapons of mass destruction. But we hold God's
promise of peace if we put God's way of nonviolence into
practice. And so we must all insist that war, nuclear weapons,
and systemic injustice be abolished. We must begin the process
in faith, knowing that God will use our small actions, multiply
their impact, and let them bear the good fruit of peace for future generations.

My friends and I were tried, found in contempt, retried,
and finally, in four separate trials, found guilty, seven months
after the initial action. Eventually, I was sentenced to several

months under house arrest and three years of supervised release, and set free from jail.

What an ordeal to stand on trial for enacting nuclear disarmament! The government and military authorities took every step they could to ensure that the jury would not agree with us, or hear the truth about these weapons of destruction, or the many international laws which outlaw them and command ordinary citizens to prevent preparations for genocide.

At the first trial, we were issued an *in limine* motion by the judge and the federal prosecutor, working together, stating that we were not allowed to discuss any of the following items: the U.S. military; nuclear weapons; international law; the Nuremberg Principles; the Necessity Defense; the U.S. government; the crimes committed by the military at the Seymour Johnson Air Force Base and other U.S. military bases; war crimes committed by the U.S. government; U.S. government foreign or domestic policies; the Bible, theology, philosophy, divine law, or natural law; and God. "Other than that, you can say whatever you like!" we were told.

We stood up, objected to this silencing of truth, protested the charade of the court which so clearly defended the legality of war and U.S. weapons of mass destruction, and were immediately found in contempt of court. The judge declared a mistrial, and we were sent back to jail. The whole episode was unnerving, if not terrifying, and yet, as we reread Jesus' court-room experiences before Caiaphas, Herod, and Pilate and re-called other trials by prisoners of conscience throughout history who spoke the unpalatable truth, we were heartened and filled with a grace that we had not experienced before.

At one point during our four separate trials, I was called to testify on behalf of Philip Berrigan, my friend and "partner in crime" who has been protesting war all his life. I sat on the wit-ness stand, right next to the judge who seemed to hate us, and the jury who seemed to think we were crazy, and looked out at the packed courtroom. "What did you see Philip Berrigan doing on December 7, 1993?" Ramsey Clark, the former U.S. Attorney General asked me on Phil's behalf.

"I saw Philip Berrigan standing up for life and peace and humanity," I responded spontaneously. "I saw him trying to tell the country that the only way out of our enormous problems is through immediate and total disarmament, so that those bil-lions of dollars spent on war and these immoral weapons could be spent on real human needs. I saw Philip Berrigan trying to stop the mass murder of war, to call us back to the sanity of peace, to uphold God's command that we beat swords into plowshares."

This was also not well received. When the prosecutor got his chance to cross-examine me, he shouted angrily, "Who drove the car?" He wanted to know who drove us to the military base, to catch others who tried to help us, and to charge them also with conspiracy to commit a felony. "I take responsibility for my own actions," I replied, refusing to give out any further information. "I accept the consequences for what I did, and will not incriminate anyone else."

The judge dismissed the jury, and told me in no uncertain terms that I was under oath, that I had to answer the question, and that if I did not, I would face additional years in prison for contempt of court.

Alright, I said. I will announce who drove us to the Seymour Johnson Air Force Base.

The jury was called back in, the crowd sat on the edge of their seats, the judge appeared delighted, and the prosecutor triumphantly asked his question again.

"Thank you for insisting that I tell the truth," I answered again spontaneously. "You have helped me by pushing me to state the truth about our action for nuclear disarmament on December 7, 1993. We've spoken a lot about truth and the need to speak the truth in court, and I want to speak the truth. And so, in all truth, we were driven to Seymour Johnson Air Force Base—by the Holy Spirit!"

The courtroom exploded. The judge yelled at me and pounded his gavel, the prosecutor shouted at me, and the spectators applauded. I was hauled out of the courtroom and my testimony stricken from the record.

Yet I felt strangely liberated. Who in their right mind would walk through a "Shoot to Kill" zone, hammer on a nuclear-capable fighter-bomber, accept the consequences for such dramatic action, endure prison, and still try to be nonviolent, contemplative, hopeful, and loving? Such nonviolent undertakings or experiments in truth, as Gandhi called them, could only come about through a life of prayer and faith. "It's not easy to walk onto a military base and call for disarmament," I said as they hauled me out in handcuffs. "Our action could only have been an act of God!" Instead of the terror I had known, I now felt exhilarated! I had spoken the truth! God wants us to disarm.

Yes, the truth shall set us free.

In the end, at my sentencing, I was allowed to make a final statement before the judge. "These weapons of mass destruction," I said, "like the cremation ovens and gas chambers in Nazi Germany, are a moral and spiritual disaster. They not only have the potential to destroy the planet, but their very existence already implies our spiritual destruction. They are our modern idols. Instead of worshiping the God of peace and life, we worship these idols of war and death. The choice before us, then, is to carry on silently, passively, in complicity with our culture's preparations for mass murder, like the dutiful Christian citizens of Nazi Germany, running their gas chambers and cremation ovens, or to speak up, break the silence, dismantle these weapons of death, call for a culture of peace and serve the God of life."

Though our action was frightening and jail was often horrible, our faith in the living God deepened, as did our trust in the truth of nonviolence. Those were difficult days, but in retrospect, I see how that fiery ordeal purified us and led us deeper into the Holy Spirit of peace. Our prayers for peace bore fruit not only in our symbolic action, not only in the subsequent public debate throughout North Carolina and across the country, but in the grace we experienced in prison and the strength we were given to endure those days. I hope that experience of prayer, faith, and nonviolent action will continue to push me beyond the culture's limitations and the nation's boundaries to the horizon of nonviolent love, to the God of peace.

When my codefendants and I finally emerged from behind bars, we realized we were already free. Despite the best efforts of the North Carolina courts and the Bureau of Prisons, we emerged totally unrehabilitated to the ways of the culture. We came out "worse than ever," ready for more, eager to give our lives for the disarmament of the world. We were filled with the spirit of God, and felt a great joy and peace that the world could never give.

I spent over ten years preparing for that action, preparing for prison, preparing to risk my life in nonviolent civil disobedience for the sake of disarmament. I know that we are only beginning to build a worldwide movement for nuclear disarmament and the abolition of war, and that great sacrifices will have to be made by thousands of people around the world in the decades to come if we are to realize the dream of peace. And though it was more than difficult, like a deep-sea plunge into the depths of despair and darkness, it was the greatest act of faith, hope, and love that I have yet experienced. I felt God's presence in our action, and God's abiding presence in the hell-hole of my jail cell. Indeed, when I entered my jail cell, it seemed like Jesus was sitting there waiting for me, saying, "Where have you been? Come on in and join me."

I realized that everything written about imprisonment for the sake of conscience and truth, from St. Paul and St. Edmund Campion to Dorothy Day and Martin Luther King, Jr., is true: God comes close to prisoners and peacemakers. If I ever feel the spirit of Peace pushing me again in that direction, I hope I will have the courage to take up the challenge, to walk that long road, to accept that cross, because I know that it opens the door to resurrection and the gift of peace.

Since 1980, there have been over sixty such "Plowshares" actions. And though not everyone is called to enter a military base to hammer on weapons of mass destruction, everyone can work for nuclear disarmament and the abolition of war.

Whether we speak out, join a peace organization, fast and

pray, hold vigils, preach, write, lobby, organize, or demonstrate for an end to war, we can all do something for peace. We can all engage in nonviolent, public action for the sake of humanity. We can all take another step toward a world without weapons and war. We can all allow God to disarm our hearts so that God's dream of a disarmed world will come true.

In the nineteenth century, when slavery was perfectly legal, many brave people risked their lives for the impossible dream of its abolition. At that time, Henry David Thoreau wrote: "If one thousand, one hundred, or if ten people whom I could name—if ten honest people only—aye, if one honest person in this state of Massachusetts, ceasing to hold slaves, were actually to withdraw from this copartnership and be locked up in the county jail, it would be the abolition of slavery in America. For it matters not how small the beginning may seem to be: what is once done well is done forever."

Likewise, our prayerful, committed actions for nuclear disarmament and the abolition of war spell the end of all weapons of mass destruction and war itself. We are witnessing the beginning of the end of war. Though these times are difficult and deadly, they are exciting and hopeful because a new time is being born.

However we put our hope for peace into practice, we all must do something. Each one of us must undertake the climb to God's mountain of peace, where we will hear God's commandment that the nations disarm, and decide to put that vision into practice and study war no more, as the prophet Isaiah foresaw long ago. His words still ring true. They show us the path to peace. They invite us to the life of peace.

Come, let us climb the mountain of God, to the house of the God of Jacob, that God may instruct us in God's ways, and we may walk in God's paths. For from Zion shall go forth instruction, and the word of God from Jerusalem. God shall judge between the nations, and impose terms on many peoples. They shall beat their swords into plowshares, and their spears into pruning hooks; one nation shall not raise the sword against another, nor shall they train for war again. (Isaiah 2:3–4)

19.

And Justice for All

The problems of the world are so enormous that most of us just throw up our hands and give up trying to make a difference. It's not just the killings, war-making, and nuclear weapons that enslave us. The entire political-economic system governing the world is structured to greatly benefit the few to the detriment of the vast majority simply struggling to survive. The top 1 percent of the world's population owns or controls most of the world's resources. While a handful squabble over how many millions to spend for the right house in the Hamptons, billions of others suffer in squalor. Because the most privileged people hoard so much of the world's resources, their countries maintain a vast arsenal of weapons to protect their status. The crisis of war and weapons arises out of this economic disparity and the desperation it spawns.

If you want peace, Pope Paul VI said famously, then you have to work for justice.

When Martin Luther King, Jr., was awarded the Nobel Peace Prize in 1964, he proclaimed his vision of a world without war, weapons, or racism, but he also made it clear that such a vision required economic justice for everyone in the world. "I have the audacity to believe that peoples everywhere can have three meals a day for their bodies, education and culture for their minds, and dignity, equality and freedom for their spirits. I believe that what self-centered men have torn down, other-centered people can build up."[12] The struggle for a world without weapons, King knew, is a struggle for economic justice and human rights.

In a world of injustice, how can we help all those who suffer? The struggle for justice requires dedication, creativity, and commitment. A wide variety of tactics employed with love, from community organizing and petitions, to vigils and boycotts, to lobbying efforts and legal battles, to demonstrations and civil disobedience, can advance the cause of justice. Gandhi, King, Nelson Mandela, and other leaders have shown how determination and perseverance will inevitably lead to greater justice. The abolitionist movement taught us that, despite the enormous opposition, even death threats, courageous actions, organizing and public witness could bring an end to slavery, a goal once deemed unreachable. The forty-year struggle to abolish South Africa's racist system of apartheid cost the lives of many courageous people, but global boycotts, nonviolent civil disobedience, and the vision of a determined people broke it down and led to a more just society.

Today there are so many areas of injustice it's hard to know where to begin. Racism, sexism, poverty, and oppression flourish around the world. We cannot personally solve every injustice, but we can't just sit back and allow injustice to continue. Whether we struggle for an end to racism or sexism, for the rights of the people of Sudan or the homeless, for an end to torture or for a living wage, we can make a positive contribution that will move us all toward social, racial, political, and economic justice.

In the last decade of the twentieth century, grassroots groups from Europe and North America have called for the cancellation of the debt of the developing world, not as a plea for charity but as a matter of justice. The burden of debt among the world's poorest nations is both morally unacceptable and economically unsustainable. The enormous interest payments alone impoverish these nations. Instead of funding healthcare, education, and agriculture, these countries pay debts and interest to privileged leaders. According to the United Nations, world debt in 1980 topped over $567 billion.

By 1992, debt grew to over $1.4 trillion. Yet with interest, developing nations paid trillions more and owe even greater amounts.

The wealthiest 20 percent of humanity owns 80 percent of the world's wealth, while the most impoverished 20 percent own only 1.4 percent of the world's wealth. No matter how hard poor nations struggle, they can never pay off the debt or even its interest. Instead, their people starve and die! In recent years, the Jubilee movement has brought thousands of ordinary Europeans and North Americans to the streets to demand the cancellation of debt, the redistribution of wealth to end starvation and destitution, and a clean slate for the new millennium.

People of faith around the world, from the Pope to community groups in rural Brazil, have invoked the Hebrew year of Jubilee. Described in the book of Leviticus, every forty-nine years all debts are canceled and land is equally redistributed. Christians note Jesus' first sermon, recorded in chapter four of Luke's Gospel, where Jesus announces that he has come "to bring good news to the poor, release to captives, sight to the blind, liberty to those who are oppressed, and to proclaim the year of jubilee." (Luke 4:18–19) In this spirit, the new millennium is seen as a unique opportunity to practice justice, declare jubilee, and cancel the debt.

In May, 1998, I participated in a daylong international protest with a diverse crowd of over 60,000 in Birmingham, England. Leaders of the eight most powerful nations were meeting to discuss trade. Every church in the city hosted workshops and lectures on world poverty, global economic structures, and alternative economics. At precisely three o'clock that afternoon, all 60,000 of us joined hands in the largest human circle of modern times, surrounding the city of Birmingham in a show of solidarity with the developing world and a commitment to the relief of debt. Surprisingly, British government officials offered to meet with movement leaders. The following year, after a similar demonstration in Scotland, the same world leaders announced they were canceling some $70 billion in debt, a critical first step toward a more just world economy. From the protests against the World Trade Organization in Seattle in 1999 to the protests against the International Monetary Fund in Washington, D.C., in 2000, the campaign continues.

Grassroots campaigns against segregation and racism throughout the twentieth century, most notably the U.S. civil rights movement, epitomized by the Montgomery bus boycott, the Birmingham protest, and the Selma march, have helped dismantle pillars of institutionalized racism. Yet there is enormous work left to do before racial and economic justice are realized. Police brutality, homelessness, and discrimination in employment, education, and healthcare must still be abolished.

In January 1999, four white New York police officers shot at an unarmed West African immigrant named Amadou Diallo forty-one times. After Amadou Diallo's death, African American leaders began a peaceful sit-in at police headquarters in Manhattan. Every day hundreds joined the protest, and scores were arrested for civil disobedience. During the first fifteen days, 1,166 religious leaders, celebrities, politicians, and activists were arrested. I joined the sit-in to lend my own voice to the call for an end to police brutality. The movement gained speedy notoriety which forced New York government officials to meet with African American leaders, and finally implement some change in policy. But we still have much work to do to ensure the rights of all, including the basic right to life.

Earlier, in the fall of 1989, I joined housing activists in Washington, D.C., to bring attention to the growing homelessness in America, and in particular, the ongoing evictions of poor people in D.C. Several of us staged a mock eviction in front of the U.S. Capitol building. We were arrested, jailed overnight, and put on trial in the spring of 1989. We spoke of our work among the homeless, explained how the local government hires homeless people to evict the poor, and testified to the need for massive government funding for decent affordable housing for all. After three days of testimony, the judge was so moved, she wept. She found us not guilty.

"The arc of the moral universe is long," Dr. King said frequently, "but it bends toward justice."

Before Jesus blessed the peacemakers, he blessed those who hunger and thirst for justice. Then, after blessing the peacemakers, he gave his last beatitude to those persecuted for the sake of justice.

The life of peace requires that we join the global struggle for justice. If every one simplifies his or her life, shares resources, condemns the hoarding of resources, resists the structures which oppress two billion people into starvation and misery, and lends a voice to the call for justice, then as the Bible says, one day, "justice will roll down like waters and righteousness like a mighty stream." When everyone has their own "vine and fig tree," then everyone will share the life of peace. Until then, while so many suffer and die from the global economic injustice, we will never rest in true peace.

20.

Including Everyone

On October 10, 1998, a young college student from Laramie, Wyoming, named Matthew Shepard was robbed, beaten, tied to a fence post in a deserted woods, and left to die—because of his sexual orientation. The following year in Texas, James Byrd was walking home one evening when he was kidnapped, assaulted, tied to a chain, and dragged behind a truck until he died—because he was African American. In April 1999, two high school students shot and killed Isaiah Shoels at Columbine High School—because he was an African American—and then they killed another thirteen students, each for some hate-filled reason. In the summer of 1999, children at a community center in Los Angeles were shot at—because they were Jewish.

Over 10,000 such hate crimes are reported in the United

States each year. On October 7, 1999, the Fellowship of Reconciliation organized over 350 "Stop the Hate" vigils around the country, at least one in every U.S. state, and several in other countries as well. Bringing together religious, community, and grassroots leaders, the vigils coalesced opposition to hate crime, raised awareness, and created communities of tolerance, respect, and inclusivity. From Portland, Maine, to Los Angeles, California, thousands gathered to listen to representatives of different groups, cultures, races, and religions to affirm the vision of an all-inclusive society. I will never forget the moving gathering in Garden City, Long Island, that brought together hundreds of people, with representatives from over fifteen religions praying, pleading, for a new kind of culture.

The life of peace excludes no one. If we wish to live at peace with ourselves, we need to accept others for who they are. We need to learn to see every other person as our own beloved sister and brother.

To begin the work of creating a culture of inclusion we must first recognize that we live in a culture of exclusion. Early on we learn to label others as "outsiders," while seeking to make ourselves "insiders." We turn our backs on so many. We exclude women and children. We exclude those whose skin color is different from our own. We exclude lesbians and gays, or the disabled, or the elderly, or people of different faith traditions. We exclude immigrants, or prisoners, or death row inmates, or the unborn, or the homeless, or refugees. And by definition, we exclude our enemies.

As we choose to exclude others and support a culture of exclusion, we tear down the web of our common humanity, erect dividing walls and sow the seeds of war and destruction.

People who embrace true peace welcome everyone. Men renounce sexism and celebrate their equality with women. Caucasians resist prejudice, oppose racism, embrace African Americans, Asian Americans, Latinos, and all people as their equals. Heterosexual people affirm the lives and rights of people of other gender preferences. People of sound physical health uphold the rights and equality of physically disabled people. Adults champion the rights of children. Young and middle-aged people respect and learn from the elderly. The faith or disbelief of individuals and groups is respected and honored. Immigrants, prisoners, people who are homeless, the poor, refugees, and people with AIDS are welcomed, and their needs are met. And we refuse the ultimate act of exclusion: We refuse to kill anyone.

Each one of us can search our heart and identify people we would choose to exclude from the human circle. Then, we can take action to include them, and root out the violence that fosters such hatred within us. We can also join local, national, and international organizations doing the same work of inclusion and reconciliation throughout the world.

Each one of us needs to break down the self-made walls we have erected to separate ourselves from those we label as "outsiders" and "inferior" to our own delusional "superiority." Through daily meditation, we can pray about those we tend to exclude, see how God does not reject or exclude us, learn to stop rejecting them, start welcoming them and everyone as a child of God, and begin to help transform society. We then participate in the reconciliation, transformation, and restoration of the whole human race.

If we truly want to welcome Jesus' "reign of God" and Martin Luther King, Jr.'s "beloved community," we need to welcome all those around us, including those the culture and we ourselves have excluded for so long. Saints, heroes, and peacemakers throughout history envisioned a new culture where no one is excluded, where everyone is welcome as sister and brother. We can, too.

How will we achieve an all-inclusive society? What would such an all-inclusive culture look like? An inclusive society will value every human being, and create structures for everyone to realize the fullness of life and dignity and equality in freedom. It will educate everyone, from kindergarten through college. It will teach nonviolence to children and young adults. It will not support, uphold, or reward racism or sexism. Instead, it will dismantle institutionalized racism and sexism, make reparations, and rigorously promote equality and dignity for everyone.

In Italy, for example, the disabled are adamantly and actively welcomed into every facet of society, beginning with grade school. The disabled are treated with extra reverence and ensured the best possible care so that they can have the most fulfilling life possible. They are valued as equal human beings who are simply differently abled. We North Americans have a long way to go to reach such inclusive values and structures.

Likewise, members of an all-inclusive society resist any and every attempt to marginalize and dehumanize others. Nazi Germany practiced genocide against Jews, gypsies, gays, the ill, the elderly, and dissenters because most German citizens looked away and silently accepted early forms of racism and exclusivity in the 1920s and 1930s. Eventually, the Nazis were able to legally categorize human beings into classes of superiority and inferiority, where some people were deemed expendable, unworthy to live, and sent to the cremation ovens. If we want to be all-inclusive, we must give our lives resisting every attempt at exclusivity, whether from the Nazis or the Ku Klux Klan or our own governments.

An all-inclusive society will accept human variety and value human difference. Following the law of nonviolence, it will not judge or condemn others but uphold every individual life. In such a culture, we will realize that there is enough room and life and space and food for everyone. We will realize that we do not have to hate anyone anymore. This will come as a great relief, and we will discover that peace and reconciliation have been granted to us long ago. We were just too blind to see it.

Many communities have attempted such all-inclusive love. Certainly the desert fathers and mothers and ancient monasteries tried in their own way, within the limitations of their times, to be welcoming, hospitable havens. St. Francis tried enthusiastically to include everyone, beginning with the most wretched, most excluded member of his society—the leper. When he served and kissed a leper himself, he realized that every human being is a child of God and that God excludes no one. From then on, he demonstrated a "preferential love for the poor and excluded," as church theologians now describe it.

Dorothy Day's Catholic Worker Houses of Hospitality also attempt to be places of welcome, where the excluded are included with great care and respect. Through soup kitchens, shelters, and farms, the Catholic Worker movement embraces all those shoved to the margins of society, and tries, in Peter Maurin's words, "to build a new society in the shell of the old." Indeed, those at the margins are now placed squarely in the center.

My mother tells a story from the 1950s, when she was a

nurse at St. Vincent's Hospital in lower Manhattan. There was one particular man who was dying, who did not have a family or any friends, and who was completely destitute.

One day, the man received a letter from Dorothy Day. He was so happy to receive it, he showed it to my mother, who shared it with other nurses and doctors. Everyone was astounded by its beauty, love, and concern.

Dorothy wrote him as if he were the Pope himself or the President or the Queen of England. For Dorothy Day, this dying, homeless man was none other than Christ himself, and deserved the best care and greatest love society could offer. With great kindness, gentleness, and compassion, she invited him to come and live and die on her Catholic Worker farm in Easton, New Jersey. "We would be honored to have you with us," Dorothy wrote, my mother remembers. "Our farm is not an institution. It is a home, and we want to welcome you to our home. We want you to be at home with us, to be a member of our family, to rest and live and die in peace surrounded by those who love you."

Dorothy Day modeled an all-inclusive love. So did Mother Teresa as she cared for the poor and dying of Calcutta. Each one of us can practice inclusive love and welcome those rejected by the culture also. As we practice inclusive love, more and more we realize the potential of our own humanity. We begin to make peace a living reality in our world. Such a transformation will not be easy, of course. As we begin to create an inclusive society that values equality and human variety, we will need mediation and nonviolent conflict-resolution skills. But the more we pursue God's justice and equality, the greater the peace we will experience together as a people. As each of us individually lets go of our judgments and exclusive tendencies, we will not only gain new sisters and brothers, we will experience greater peace within us. Our lives will be transformed, our minds broadened, and our hearts enlarged.

Finally, we are learning what it means to be a human being: to welcome every other human being as an equal child of God; to love and serve everyone equally with all our hearts; to be people of nonviolence who worship a God of nonviolence and reflect God's reign of nonviolence by creating here and now a culture of nonviolence.

As we put this new all-inclusive love into practice, and make God's reign more present here on earth, we realize more and more that we will never be excluded by God but welcomed along with everyone else into God's all-inclusive home. Instead of waiting for some distant heaven after our death, we desire with all our hearts to put that love into practice now, and in doing so, create a taste of heaven here on earth.

III.

The Horizons of Peace

*If we want to reap the harvest of peace and justice in the future,
we will have to sow seeds of nonviolence, here and now, in the present.*

MAIREAD CORRIGAN MAGUIRE,
NOBEL PEACE LAUREATE FROM BELFAST

*The job of the peacemaker is to stop war, to purify the world, to get it
saved from poverty and riches, to heal the sick, to comfort the sad, to
wake up those who have not yet found God, to create joy and beauty
wherever you go, and to find God in everything and in everyone.*

MURIEL LESTER

*When the practice of nonviolence becomes universal,
God will reign on earth as God does in heaven.*

MAHATMA GANDHI

21

Love Your Enemies

I f we seek to live a life of peace, then we need to learn to love everyone, even our enemies. As I write this, the greatest perceived enemy of the United States is still Iraq. If we want to live in peace, we must learn to love the people of Iraq.

In March 1999, I led a Fellowship of Reconciliation delegation to Iraq that included Nobel Peace Prize laureates Mairead Corrigan Maguire of Northern Ireland and Adolfo Pérez Esquivel of Argentina. Throughout our visit, the U.S. bombed Iraq daily, killing civilians with U.S. F15-E fighter-bombers, like the bomber I disarmed during my 1993 "Plowshares" action.

With a population of 23.5 million people, Iraq was once a prosperous nation with first-rate medical and educational facilities. When the United Nations and the United States imposed harsh economic sanctions on Iraq on August 6, 1990, they also began years of bombardments, systematically destroying Iraq's infrastructure and killing its people. The United States claims that it is trying to bring down a dictator. None of us supports the violence of Saddam Hussein, but the actual effect of U.S. policy throughout the 1990s has *not* been to promote democracy, but to kill more Iraqis, especially children, and destroy the land. The U.S. policy toward Iraq has been a total failure.

According to UNICEF and the World Health Organization, over one million Iraqi civilians died during the 1990s as a result of economic sanctions. Most of the dead are children under the age of five. About six thousand children die each month because of economic sanctions—approximately two hundred children a day. One million Iraqi children under five are chronically malnourished. Not only are food and medicine in severely short supply, but water supplies are contaminated, and the sanitation and sewage systems have been destroyed. Even if the children can be healed, they quickly get sick again. Disease cycles relentlessly whether it is prevented or not. The United States government has declared war on the children of Iraq.

On February 12, 1991, on the last day of Ramadan, which was also Ash Wednesday, the Ameriyah shelter in Baghdad was filled with some 1,200 women, children and elderly men seeking shelter and celebrating these holidays as well as a birthday.

In the early hours of the morning, a U.S. "smart" bomb entered the ventilation shaft, blew open the ceiling, threw seventeen people outside, forced the exits closed, and trapped everyone inside. Minutes later, a second "smart" bomb entered the ceiling hole and incinerated everyone inside within seconds.

One woman, Umm Greyda, had gone out to do laundry for her nine children and other relatives. She survived the bombing, and later moved into the shelter to create a permanent memorial to the victims of the massacre.

After crossing the border and passing through the Iraqi desert, our delegation drove directly to Baghdad, to the Ameriyah shelter. Umm Greyda welcomed us, described the horrific event, and led us through the shelter. The massive concrete structure reminded me of the Sacred Heart Center, the women and children's center in Richmond, Virginia. Its concrete walls are charred black. Now flowers, written prayers, and pictures of martyred children crowd the walls. We walked through the shelter in shock. We saw where children on the top bunks had clawed the ceiling to escape, leaving only charred hand prints behind.

On one wall, we could see the outline of a woman incinerated. The whole wall was charcoal black except for a lighter area where she had been standing. Her arm is outstretched, pointing. Another light shadow outlined a mother holding a child.

We gathered below the mammoth hole where the bombs entered. It is no exaggeration to say that what we were seeing was similar to the worst human suffering in history, at places such as Hiroshima and even Auschwitz. Umm Greyda told us the killings continue each day, as thousands die from U.S./U.N. economic sanctions. On behalf of the Fellowship of Reconciliation, I expressed profound sorrow, asked forgiveness, and pledged to work for an end to the killing. I presented Umm Greyda with over a thousand signed FOR statements, "A Covenant of Peace with the People of Iraq," from religious congregations across the U.S. We joined hands. Adolfo led us in prayer for an end to the U.S. bombings and economic sanctions. We wept. We embraced. We took a deep breath, and drove into Baghdad. Our journey was only beginning.

We met with representatives of Iraqi nongovernmental organizations, U.N. officials in Baghdad, government officials, including Tarik Aziz, and afterward, with Queen Noor of Jordan. We heard detailed reports about the devastation and massive loss of life resulting from the economic sanctions. "A whole generation has been destroyed," one Iraqi woman solemnly told me.

At the Dijla Primary School, hundreds of young girls greeted us with flowers and sang an Arabic rendition of the classic civil rights anthem, "We Shall Overcome." "We are not afraid," they sang. "We'll walk hand in hand . . . Deep in our hearts, we do believe, that we shall live in peace someday."

The students told us their experiences of war and sanctions. "Why is your government bombing us?" several asked with uncontrollable emotion. "Why are you killing us? We want to live in love and friendship and peace with Americans." The principal told us of the fear and terror that afflicted the students during the December 1998 bombardment of Baghdad by U.S. warplanes. We hugged the children, took their photos, and promised to do what we could to build peace.

But the worst was yet to come. At the Al Mansour Pediatrics Hospital, the hospital director, doctors, and nurses all told us that seven children die each day there for lack of medicine, equipment, electricity, and clean water. "The death rate is increasing, although we do our best to reverse it," the director explained.

Before our eyes we saw the cruelty of economic sanctions. We walked from bed to bed, holding the hands of dying children, embracing weeping mothers in black, listening to the pleas of doctors. For a long time, Mairead held a crying child, dying of kidney cancer and severe birth defects, with her arm around the mother.

Adolfo and I met Sara, a six-year-old girl with cancer, who was so depressed that she had stopped eating. We listened to her, told her that we work for peace, and asked her to eat for us. We promised to keep working. Finally, she agreed. But Adolfo said we couldn't leave until she smiled, and slowly, a heartbreaking smile spread across her beautiful face.

The doctors pointed out the sharp rise in cancers and birth defects, especially in the south, near Basra, due to contamination from U.S. bombings and depleted uranium.

"These children are innocent people," the director exclaimed passionately. "They are not hurting the U.S. or Britain. They are not violating your air space. They have a right to food, medicine, and clean water. They ask to live their lives peacefully, normally. Please, let them live."

In Iraq, I visited a Calvary, where Christ is tortured and dies over and over again in the guise of children on the cross of U.S. economic sanctions, his grieving mother in black at his side. We were shaken, disturbed, traumatized.

"We would like to wish you a happy visit to Iraq," a researcher at the Umm 'Amarik Research Center told us. "But we are a suffering and dying people, and if you come to Baghdad, you will suffer with us. Tell the world that Iraqis are being suffocated in silence. These economic sanctions are as harmful to us as nuclear weapons."

After meeting with Christian and Muslim leaders, we held a press conference to report our findings. "We call for the immediate lifting of the economic sanctions, an end to the U.S.

bombings of Iraq and nonviolent resolutions to this crisis," I began.

"This is genocide," Adolfo explained. "Children are dying slowly and painfully. If we want democracy and human rights in Iraq, we have to stop the economic sanctions which kill people and destroy all educational and social services."

Mairead spoke with great emotion: "President Clinton and the United States should seek peace with Iraq just as he helped forge the 1998 Good Friday peace agreement in Northern Ireland. We in Ireland are grateful for what he has accomplished with the help of Prime Minister Blair. But he should be consistent in his call for dialogue and disarmament as the only way to make peace. He needs to stop the economic sanctions and bombings of Iraq, and dialogue with Iraq. In fifty years," she concluded, "people will ask, what were you doing when the children of Iraq were dying?"

To make peace in our world, we need to reach out to our country's enemies, see them as the sisters and brothers they are, and love and protect them as our own. Since my trip to Iraq, I have worked with greater dedication against the morally bankrupt U.S. policy that is destroying Iraq, to promote healing and reconciliation with a beautiful people. While I would never support the violence and oppression of the Iraqi regime (which may itself be responsible for killing some 150,000 Iraqis), my own responsibility requires me to help stop the violence and oppression of my own government (which has killed well over 1.1 million Iraqis since 1990).

This work has included organizing prayer vigils, letter-writing campaigns, lobbying, fasts, and press conferences about Iraq. On August 6, 2000, the tenth anniversary of the Iraq sanctions, and the fifty-fifth anniversary of the U.S. atomic bombing of Hiroshima, the Fellowship of Reconciliation and many other grassroots peace organizations, held an interfaith vigil, march, and rally at the White House that drew a diverse crowd of nearly two thousand people calling for the end of these sanctions. That same week, FOR placed a large advertisement in the *New York Times*, asking, "Are the children of Iraq our enemies?" and demanding an immediate end to the sanctions. Many well-known friends added their names to this plea for peace, including Susan Sarandon, Martin Sheen, Liam Neeson, Joan Baez, Rosie O'Donnell, Tim Robbins, Jeremy Irons, Richard Gere, Jackson Browne, Bonnie Raitt, and Ed Asner.

This work of peace and reconciliation is fundamentally not political. Though it may upset others when we reach across invisible boundaries to our country's enemies, we are simply practicing a biblical commandment. We are enacting our spiritual beliefs.

Prayer and meditation can push us beyond the limits we place on our capacity to love, and open us to love everyone, including ourselves, our families and friends, our neighbors, those we encounter in our day to day lives, the poor and oppressed, and most challenging of all, our enemies.

Love is "the hidden ground of our human existence," Thomas Merton wrote. It is the essence of life. We cannot experience the fullness of love without embracing our enemies. Only in doing so can we test the depths of the soul.

So what does it mean to love Saddam Hussein, a person currently labeled as the number-one enemy of the United States?

At the height of World War II, A. J. Muste, the director of the Fellowship of Reconciliation, organized a famous debate on war at Carnegie Hall in New York City. In the course of the evening, he told the packed audience, "As a Christian, if I cannot love Hitler, I cannot love anyone." His statement was deeply challenging and publicly explosive, but fit right in with the life and teachings of Jesus.

Likewise, today, if we cannot love Saddam Hussein, or any other government leader, we cannot love anyone. What does it mean to love Saddam Hussein? It means nonviolently resisting U.S. government plans to kill him and his people; and then likewise challenging him to stop his own oppressive violence. While I was in Iraq, our delegation met with Iraqi government leaders and we told them of our commitment to stop the deadly U.S. economic sanctions on Iraq, our insistence that the only way to serve one another or resist imperial might is through active nonviolence, and our desire that the Iraqi government become nonviolent and democratic. I think our message was taken much more seriously because we are consistent in our nonviolence. In any case, real love for one's enemies does not mean that we blindly, naively support their violence and do whatever they want. We do not support violence by anyone! We do try to love everyone, and that love requires speaking the truth to everyone on all sides of all conflicts. It means we keep our enemies, including Saddam Hussein, in our prayers for their healing, protection, and conversion, just as we pray for our persecutors and all people of the world.

How do we love our neighbors? What concrete public steps can we take to love those labeled as enemies? What can we do to serve, defend, and heal the children of Iraq?

The Greeks had three words for love: *eros*, or sexual love; *philia*, or love of one's friends and country people; and *agape*, or unconditional, sacrificial love for all humanity. When the Gospels cite Jesus' command to love God, neighbor, and enemies, they always use *agape*, selfless, humble, all-encompassing love. *Agape* means that we let go of our selfishness and open our arms to every human being on the planet. It calls us to heartfelt service, especially toward those who cannot repay us. It can even call us to suffer and die for others without hatred or vengeance.

The love that Jesus calls us to live has no conditions.

Though we may protest that such love is impossible, the Christian scriptures summon us to it. As we try to demonstrate real acts of love, especially toward our enemies, we gain inner strength. The grace of God works within us, works through us, to heal our sisters and brothers, and transform ourselves.

Jesus' teachings have the power to transform the world—to end wars, to make visible the nonviolent reign of God on earth—if we would only take them seriously and try to fulfill them. When we love our enemies, when we practice *agape* toward them, we become more like God. Then "you will be children of your heavenly God, for God makes God's sun rise on the bad and the good and causes rain to fall on the just and the unjust," Jesus explains in the Sermon on the Mount. "For if you love those who love you," he continues, "what recompense will you have? Do not the tax collectors do the same. And if you greet your brothers and sisters only, what is unusual about that? Do not the pagans do the same? So be compassionate, just as your heavenly God is compassionate" (Matthew 5:44–48).

Our God practices unconditional love, and since we are God's children, Jesus concludes, we must strive to do the same. It is as simple as that.

We cannot just wait around for someone else to do it. We have a certain responsibility for all our sisters and brothers, including our enemies. We are not called to save the world, but we are called to love our enemies, to do what we can to protect them. Failure to do so is not only a sin of omission; it is the opposite of love: it is an act of indifference.

When we take this call to heart, we may very well find ourselves embroiled in public turmoil, the object of ridicule, but in exchange we will experience a deep inner peace. The God of the whole human race will take our love and transform us all.

Not only can our love help save our enemies, like the beautiful children of Iraq, it can save us as well.

22.

Building Community

We cannot pursue a life of peace alone. Our culture is so violent and broken, and we too are so violent and broken, that we need the support of friends to live. Otherwise, our own violence can crush us.

If we want to spend our lives making peace in a war-torn world, we need to get together and build a community.

As in Alcoholics Anonymous, each of us needs a safe community of friends where we can confess our violence and brokenness, receive a warm welcome, be encouraged, turn back to our Higher Power, and find hope and strength to go on. With support, we can withstand whatever challenges arise.

When I committed to the journey of faith and nonviolence, I knew that I needed community. I felt called to the solitary life of celibacy, but I knew that I could not sustain such a life on my own. If I was to minister in the church, I had to have the steadfast support, care, and encouragement of a faith-filled, loving community.

I have lived in fourteen Jesuit communities around the country since I joined the Society of Jesus in 1982. From Washington, D.C., to Oakland, New York City to Virginia, El Salvador to Northern Ireland, I have lived in community, a difficult, challenging, and always blessed experience. In community, as we share our lives and serve one another, we experience moments of grace, filled with the loving presence of God in our midst.

As the years go by, I find I need community more and more, including the experience of community among peace and justice groups across the country. In these grassroots communities, I find renewed energy and new friends who enrich my life.

If we want to live a life of peace, we need to risk new relationships. Widening the circle of communities that resist war and injustice, we expand the whole peace movement and together sound a stronger and clearer voice. Our lives bear more fruit than when we work alone.

Jesus understood the importance of community. After his baptism and solitary sojourn of prayer in the desert, Jesus quickly formed a community of friends around him. This was his first public act. He invited his friends to join him on his journey. Eventually, he formalized a circle of twelve friends and missioned them to form other communities. With this circle of friends, he shared his contemplative life, his vision of God, his love, his prayer, and his very being.

Without intimate companionship, Jesus' example may have died with him on the cross. Jesus also knew that he needed community. In his human existence, he discovered the beauty of friendship, the joy of celebration, and the peace of fellowship with others. Community was at the heart of his prayer: "that all may be one."

All the great saints believed in the power of community. St. Ignatius' community, the Companions of Jesus, regularly shared "spiritual conversation." Each day, they took time to talk about God, Jesus, Mary, the Gospels, and the Holy Spirit. They were devout men of prayer. They spent rich hours in silent meditation, Bible study, readings of the Psalms, Eucharist, and reflection on life together in this world. As they shared their experiences of God with one another, they grew spiritually and they found strength from within their community to reach out to others.

Our life today, as recent Jesuit documents state, is life in "a community of brothers, who hold all things in common, who serve others and follow Jesus together." Together we "search for the will of God by means of a shared reflection on the signs which point where the Spirit of Christ is leading." We Jesuits strive to share our contemplative prayer with one another, so

that we can better follow not our will but the will of God and
the spirit of God moving in the world. This ideal is not easy to
fulfill. It is a daily struggle. And generally speaking, we don't
just fall short of this ideal, we regularly fall flat on our faces.
But this struggle is interrupted by moments of grace! And our
journey together is rich with blessings.

History's great peacemakers surrounded themselves with
community. St. Francis founded his "Order of Friars Minor" to
wander in poverty, preach the Gospel, and live together as
brothers. Dorothy Day formed the Catholic Worker "to make
it easier for people to be good." Mahatma Gandhi created his
first ashram in Durban, South Africa, not long after he visited
a Trappist monastery and saw the transforming power of life in
community. Though Thomas Merton hungered for deep solitude, eventually moving into the woods and living as a hermit,
he remained rooted to his monastic community and the reality of human relationships. He knew that without them, he
would be lost.

But good community life does not just fall from the sky. It
requires constant hard work and generosity. It is a daily struggle. As your companions discover your faults and weaknesses,
and confront you to correct them and help you grow, it can be
humiliating. Community demands regular engagement with
people whom you would otherwise just avoid. It requires loving and serving those around you. As we pray together, share

our hearts and lives with each other, we also learn to forgive one another, let go of our resentments, respect one another, and care for one another. Though community living is demanding and at times frustrating, it offers moments of pure grace, even revelation.

If a community is to grow, its members must fully share their lives with one another. Community life demands care, active listening to one another, and patient presence, especially when a community member is hurting. Communities flourish when their members regularly break bread, celebrate their joys, take risks for justice and peace, share their pain, and forgive one another.

Most of all, communities blossom when members share their personal experiences of God. We may live, eat, work, and share our resources together, but without revealing our contemplative love, we might as well be strangers staying at the Holiday Inn. When community members share their encounters with God, they enter into sacred space. As we share our intimate relationships with God, we deepen the human bonds between us, and experience a new and richer peace. In the process, God is revealed. As God moves in our communities, our communities strengthen. They offer newness of life. In moments of grace, we understand that it is God who creates and sustains us, and we are freed.

The challenge of community life, then, is to risk together

disarming our individual hearts, and creating a circle of dis-armed hearts that grows wider and wider and slowly widens to welcome the world.

Each of us can create a community of peace around us. Our families can be communities of nonviolent love, if we take care to honor, respect, and serve one another. The work-place can become a community, if each person strives to show kindness and respect to one another. The university or hospi-tal or any other institution can become a community of peace and service, if people strive intentionally to create a human atmosphere of peace and service. But each of us needs to build a community. And if we want to pursue the life of faith all our days, we will find it helpful in the long run to join a local faith community in our church or synagogue or mosque, so that we have friends to pray with, share our journey, and help us to sustain our faith during the times of struggle and doubt. As we deepen our love for all the members of our var-ious communities, we create a "community of the heart," as Henri Nouwen described it, that we take with us into God's community.

The whole world benefits from the peace created in com-munity. Communities touch communities that touch other communities around the world, creating a global community of peace.

We cannot live without one another. By living and working together, we can experience not only the fullness of life, but the gift of God's peace among us. Life in community leads to peace. All those who seek the fullness of peace will want to experiment with community life. From my own experience, I know they will ultimately not be disappointed.

23

Forgive Seventy Times Seven

L ife is an adventure in forgiveness," Norman Cousins once wrote.

If we want to find inner peace, we must forgive those who hurt us. As we forgive those who hurt us, we can forgive ourselves. We become reconciled, the bonds of common humanity are restored, and we widen the community of peace around us.

Peacemakers understand the two fundamentals of forgiveness: We are forgiven, and so we are called to forgive.

When we experience intimate prayer with God, we live not only God's love for us, but God's forgiveness for our failure to love. God loves us as we are and remains faithful to us. We, on the other hand, reject God time and time again. As we turn away from God, we turn away from our true selves and one another. We become alienated and violent. But God sees through our brokenness to the possibility of our redemption and loves us still. As we experience God's forgiveness for us, we can find strength to go forward and forgive one another.

In prayer, we do not meet a resentful God. We do not feel hatred, wrath, or vengeance from God. Rather a vulnerable God loves us with unconditional love. God is always ready to forgive, always ready to make peace, always ready to welcome us.

Throughout the Gospels, Jesus calls us to forgive one another. Peter asks, "Lord, if my brother or sister sins against me, how often must I forgive them? As many as seven times?" Jesus answers, "I say to you, not seven times but seventy times seven" (Matthew 18:21–22). When the disciples ask Jesus how to pray, he teaches them to say: "Forgive us our debts as we forgive our debtors" (Matthew 6:12). Luke sums up Jesus' path to peace with the simple call: "Forgive and you will be forgiven" (Luke 6:37).

When the crowd brings Jesus a paralytic to be healed, he tells him, "Your sins have been forgiven" (Matthew 9:2; Mark 2:5; Luke 5:20). When a woman of "ill repute" kisses Jesus' feet, bathes them in tears, wipes them with her hair, and anoints them with ointment, Jesus tells Simon the Pharisee: "Her many sins have been forgiven; hence, she has shown great love. But the one to whom little is forgiven, loves little." Then he said to her, "Your sins are forgiven" (Luke 7:47–48).

Hours before his arrest and execution, Jesus gathers his friends for the Passover meal, takes the cup reserved for Elijah's return, and declares: "Drink from it, all of you, for this is my blood of the covenant, which will be shed on behalf of all for the forgiveness of sins" (Matthew 26:27–28). He understands his death as an act of redemption. When they crucify him, Jesus says, "Father, forgive them; they know not what they do" (Luke 23:34). After his resurrection, he appears to the disciples, and speaks of peace, community and forgiveness. "Receive the Holy Spirit," he says. "Whose sins you forgive are forgiven them; those you retain together as a community are retained" (John 20:22–23).

Because we are a people forgiven by a loving God, we are a people who can forgive one another. From the daily hurts of interpersonal relationships to the horror of murder to the systemic injustice of war, we are constantly presented with opportunities to forgive. Murder and war, in fact, represent the final refusal to forgive. To become a forgiving people, we must renounce every form of violence, from hatred, vengeance, and character assassination to the death penalty, war, and nuclear weapons. We must apologize for the pain we have caused. We must believe in redemption and reconciliation. From now on, we try to reach out first with love. We forgive those who hurt us or our loved ones. We forgive even our enemies.

In the summer of 1985, I visited war-torn Nicaragua, at the

height of the U.S.–backed "contra" war. I arrived shortly after the brutal mercenary contras, set up, funded, and directed by the CIA, massacred a group of young men in the town of Estelli. At the memorial service for the youth, I approached a Nicaraguan woman whose son had been killed. As a white North American, I stood out in the crowd. I apologized to her. She looked into my eyes, embraced me, and forgave me. At that moment, through her, I knew God's far-reaching love. Her love surely came from deep faith and daily prayer. Though I was her enemy, she loved me, and I was healed. That moment was a sacrament, a gift of the Spirit. Such forgiveness sows the seeds of peace, not just between individuals, but between warring nations.

How does one forgive? After the initial sadness and anger have subsided, after we have acknowledged our pain, we can turn to God and ask for the grace to forgive. In prayer, we rediscover Jesus' unconditional love. We remember that we have hurt others, that we have rejected God, and that God still forgives us. We feel a new compassion. We understand: God forgives through us!

One of today's most dramatic stories of forgiveness is told from Northern Ireland. At the height of "the Troubles," on November 8, 1987, the IRA blew up a building along the crowded Remembrance Day parade route in Enniskillen. Gordon Wilson and his daughter, Marie, a nurse, were buried in the rubble.

Holding hands under six feet of masonry, they comforted each other. Marie whispered, "Daddy, I love you very much," then lost consciousness. She died several hours later. Ten others died that Sunday morning, and many more were seriously injured.

That night, the BBC interviewed Gordon Wilson at his home, shortly after he returned from the hospital. "The hospital was magnificent, truly impressive, and our friends have been great," he said, "but I have lost my daughter, and we shall miss her. I bear no ill will. I bear no grudge. Dirty sort of talk is not going to bring her back to life. She's in heaven, and we'll meet again. Don't ask me, please, for a purpose. I don't have a purpose. I don't have an answer. But I know there has to be a plan. If I didn't think that, I would commit suicide. It's part of a greater plan, and God is good, and we shall meet again."[13]

Gordon Wilson's refusal to retaliate or call for vengeance shocked and moved the nation. In a land simmering with centuries of resentment, his public forgiveness was a profound act of faith. In the years following, until his death from cancer in the mid-1990s, Gordon Wilson became a wise teacher of forgiveness, traveling the world, telling his story, urging others to let go of hatred and take the higher ground.

"Our Lord taught us to pray, 'Forgive us our sins, as we forgive those who sin against us,' " Wilson later wrote. "We ask God to forgive us, but we are always subject to his condition that we must forgive others. God's forgiveness is ultimate, ours is the forgiveness of person to person. To me, the two become one. It's as simple and yet as profound as that. My words were not intended as a statement of theology or of righteousness, rather they were from the heart, and they expressed exactly how I felt at the time and still do. Countless sermons have been preached on the subject of forgiveness and many books written. I do not pretend to understand all of them, since they sometimes seem to be contradictory. I prefer my conception of the simple, uncomplicated, and yet so demanding words of Christ in the Lord's Prayer."[14]

One afternoon in 1998, while I was living for a year in Northern Ireland, I traveled to Enniskillen to meet Joan Wilson, Gordon's wife and Marie's mother. We sat in her living room sipping tea, talking about peace. I asked her how she and her husband came to forgive those who killed their beloved daughter. "We knew that if we did not forgive the killers, we could never pray the Lord's Prayer again," she told me. "And we always prayed that prayer together. We wanted to continue to pray that prayer. Forgiveness was very hard, but it was the natural, right thing to do."

"We must develop and maintain the capacity to forgive," Martin Luther King, Jr., wrote. "The one who is devoid of the power to forgive is devoid of the power to love. Forgiveness is not an occasional act," King concluded. "It is a permanent attitude."[15]

Archbishop Desmond Tutu of South Africa understands this. While chairing South Africa's historic Truth and Reconciliation Commission, he concluded "there is no future without forgiveness." His commission has led South Africa toward a new level of forgiveness that wields the power to teach the world, to transform cultures, peoples, and nations.

As Gordon Wilson, Dr. King, and Archbishop Tutu demonstrated, prayer helps us to forgive. It nurtures a forgiving spirit within us. Because the contemplative peacemaker knows that God is standing beside us inviting us to forgive, we can go forward and forgive those who hurt us. The contemplative peacemaker knows that forgiveness is another essential requirement of the life of peace.

Forgiveness is an act of faith in God, an act of hope in the future, and an act of love for our neighbors. If we dare forgive, we can trust that God will deepen within and among us the gift of peace.

24.

Persistent Reconciliation

In 1914, a group of Christians met at an ecumenical conference in Germany to try to find a way to prevent the out-
break of war. They were too late. The Great War was declared
just as the gathering concluded. Standing together at the train
station, before departing, two participants—Friedrich Sig-
mund-Schültze, a German Lutheran, and Henry Hodgkin, an
English Quaker—shook hands and pledged to work together
for peace and reconciliation, even though their countries were
at war. They called for another ecumenical conference, and the
Fellowship of Reconciliation was born.

Throughout the next century, up to this day, the Fellowship of Reconciliation has worked to bring together people on
all sides in all the conflicts of the world, in pursuit of peace and
reconciliation. During World War I, FOR aided and obtained
legal recognition for conscientious objectors. They organized

the National Civil Liberties Bureau, now known as the American Civil Liberties Union (ACLU). FOR started a wide variety of campaigns—sending delegations around the world, offering solidarity with the people of Nicaragua, the Middle East, and China, teaching people the creative alternatives of nonviolence. FOR "Ambassadors of Reconciliation" met with world leaders, encouraging nonviolent solutions to conflict. During World War II, FOR led the struggle against the internment of Japanese Americans. European FOR members sheltered Jews and other political refugees from the Nazis. Some were killed by the Nazis for their resistance to fascism. Others organized international support for Gandhi's nonviolent struggle for India's independence. FOR also worked hard to stop the Pentagon from extending wartime conscription.

In the 1940s, FOR helped form the Congress of Racial Equality and set up "Journeys of Reconciliation," which promoted integration in the segregated South. Throughout the 1950s and 1960s, FOR played a vital role in the civil rights movement, working closely with Martin Luther King, Jr., during the Montgomery bus boycott, organizing workshops on nonviolence throughout the South, and bringing religious leaders into the struggle for racial equality. Early on, it launched a campaign for nuclear disarmament, organizing protests in New York City against nuclear air raid drills. In the 1960s, it launched "Shelters for the Shelterless" program, building shelters for the homeless instead of succumbing to demands for bomb shelters.

During the Vietnam War, FOR mobilized thousands of antiwar protesters. It formed the International Committee of Conscience on Vietnam, with members from over forty countries. FOR raised money for medical aid to both sides in the conflict, and sponsored a world tour of Vietnamese Buddhist monk, Thich Nhat Hanh. In the 1970s, FOR focused on the Cold War and the nuclear arms race. During the 1980s, FOR initiated U.S.-USSR reconciliation programs, and cofounded the Freeze antinuclear campaign. In 1985, FOR led extensive nonviolence training seminars in the Philippines, a year before the nonviolent "People Power" movement helped mobilize the overthrow of the Marcos dictatorship.

During the 1990s, FOR opposed U.S. military action against Iraq, sent delegations to Iraq to try to stop the Gulf War and later bombings, and worked diligently to lift the economic sanctions on Iraq. FOR also worked to stop the NATO bombings of Yugoslavia in 1999. In 1994, FOR initiated the Bosnia Student Project, bringing over 150 Bosnian youth out of war zones and into U.S. homes and schools. For years, FOR led annual Bosnian Reconciliation Work Camps, where people from all faiths on all sides of the war-torn Balkans worked together over the course of several intensive weeks to rebuild damaged villages. While opposing U.S. wars in Central America and apartheid in South Africa, FOR worked throughout the 1990s to ensure U.S. military withdrawal from Panama, and to expose U.S. chemical weapons there.

Today, FOR continues to work to abolish nuclear weapons and war, to demilitarize the U.S. presence in Latin America, to promote racial and economic justice, and to promote the newly declared United Nations' "Decade for a Culture of Peace and Nonviolence, 2001–2010." FOR hosts peacemaker training institutes for young people, and educates and protests against hate crimes, racism, and the death penalty. We lead peacemaking delegations to war zones around the world, and inform people about issues of peace and justice through our national magazine, *Fellowship*.

After nearly a century of dedicated peacemaking, members of the Fellowship of Reconciliation remain as committed as ever to the mission of promoting peace, justice, and nonviolent action. Never was the work of interfaith peacemaking more urgently needed. Whether the cause is popular or not, the persistent work of reconciliation continues.

What have we learned? FOR is learning the great wisdom of the ages: that making peace requires persistent reconciliation. Peace does not happen overnight. There is no immediate result. It is a lifelong struggle, and requires a lifetime commitment. It necessitates patience and dedication, even facing the worst odds. The challenge of reconciliation is to keep at it—to keep opponents talking, to encourage compassionate listening, to invite forgiveness, to compromise for the sake of peace, and to never give up the dream. It requires committed organizing across the country at the grassroots level to build a movement for nonviolent social change.

When FOR moved from being exclusively Christian to truly interfaith in the late 1950s, it broadened its mission to include building bridges between all the world's religions for the sake of peace. Today, FOR embraces Christians, Jews, Muslims, Buddhists, Hindus, other people of faith, and those with no formal religious affiliation. Through this interfaith commitment to nonviolence, we are forging a modest, new path into a new future for us all.

In November 1999, I experienced just one of countless experiments in nonviolence and reconciliation that we have engaged in over the years. I journeyed with an interfaith FOR delegation to Palestine and Israel, and saw firsthand the historic demands and work of reconciliation. Some call this land the most divided region in the world. We heard firsthand accounts of violence, house demolitions, imprisonments, and military occupation by Israelis upon Palestinians. Yet with Jewish and Muslim friends, I met dedicated Israelis and Palestinians determined to resolve their conflicts nonviolently. They continue to advocate an end to these human rights abuses, land seizures, and violence, and call for a peaceful future, even as the crisis worsens.

In Neve Shalom, we met Israelis and Palestinians who live together in an intentional village, raising children together, praying together, speaking equally both Arabic and Hebrew, and dreaming together about creating a new kind of society based on respect, equality, and reconciliation. Though violence and turmoil continue to tear apart this sacred land, their risky work for justice and reconciliation along with the efforts of other pioneers of nonviolence will bear good fruit someday in the future. Their work of reconciliation, though difficult and frustrating now demonstrates the possibility of peace and offers future generations somewhere down the road an opportunity for real peace.

FOR and many other nongovernmental organizations that promote peace and reconciliation carry on their work quietly, modestly, and steadfastly, largely ignored by governments and the media. Though we wish the whole world would embark on the journey of persistent reconciliation, we know we cannot rely on consistent and fair media coverage to make it happen. The work of peace and reconciliation is not only political, it's human work, and it's spiritual. The God of peace is determined to reconcile the human race, and employs whomever will help in this great project. Some of us need to systematically work together, in organizations like FOR, to build and support the movements for peace and justice that cooperate with God's transformation of the world. Whatever peace organization we join, I hope everyone will get involved with a local and national peace group.

As we have seen from the abolitionist, suffragist, civil rights, antiwar, human rights, and environmental movements, patient grassroots organizing and reconciliation over time has the power to transform nations and the world.

I believe that if we want to explore the horizons of peace, we need to join with organizations and nonviolent movements striving to transform the world. As we add our voices to these programs and sow the seeds of peace and reconciliation, we become part of a movement larger than ourselves, and thus take our part in history's journey to peace.

25.

Hope upon Hope

O n December 31, 1999, the eve of the new millennium, five hundred of us gathered in bitter cold weather around a roaring bonfire in the middle of the Nevada desert, sixty-five miles north of Las Vegas. With the majestic desert mountains around us and a sky full of stars overhead, we listened to a Native American Shoshone spiritual leader explain how the U.S. government has been exploding nuclear weapons on their land since 1951, permanently radiating the land and killing plant and animal life. After he offered a prayer for the healing of the earth and a Catholic bishop blessed us, we lit candles from the bonfire, lined up in pairs, and proceeded a mile and a half to the entrance of the Nevada test site.

We had been meeting for several days on the theme "Walking the Ways of Peace." With each step through the desert, I took in a deep breath and felt a great inner calm. The sky, the cold night air, the flickering candle, the desert floor, and the community spirit among us combined to send shivers down our spines. We were trying to walk the way of peace and since we were walking toward the U.S. nuclear weapons test site entrance to arrive at the stroke of midnight, at the dawn of a new millennium, we felt we were walking into the future. We were sure it would be a future of peace.

In other words, we were filled with hope.

Scores of armed soldiers stood facing us as we approached the line. Actor Martin Sheen knelt down and led us in the Lord's Prayer. Just at midnight, 331 of us walked onto the base in an act of peaceful civil disobedience to begin the new millennium with a call for disarmament and peace. It was a moment of grace, an epiphany of nonviolence, a beautiful start to the new century. We all felt transformed by the experience, filled with the spirit of peace.

Earlier that evening, Jonathan Schell, author of the groundbreaking book, *The Fate of the Earth*, pointed out that with the end of the Cold War, we have an historic opportunity to abolish nuclear weapons from the face of the earth. Though we have failed to seize the moment; though we maintain our arsenal, develop new weapons of mass destruction, block any movement toward disarmament, even vote down the Comprehensive Test Ban treaty; though nuclear proliferation and the real threat of nuclear war between nations like

Pakistan and India have brought us again to the brink of danger, still God has given us the opportunity to disarm ourselves and live in peace. We still have a chance to change our world. We still have reason for hope.

"One nuclear weapon can kill millions of people," Schell said. "We have many thousands of them. It is wrong to have these weapons. It will always be wrong. Abolishing nuclear weapons is the right thing to do, and it's the right time to do it, and it is necessary for us to do it. We still have a chance to guarantee peace for future generations. Now more than ever is the time to speak out for nuclear disarmament." His charge emboldened us to take the fateful step across the line into the new millennium.

We were arrested and held in an outdoors fenced-in area for several hours. Later the charges were dropped.

The challenge to remain hopeful in the face of the violence in ourselves and our world is perhaps the greatest challenge of all. And yet this is precisely the definition of hope: to carry on strong in the spirit of truth and love despite all the evidence pointing to failure and defeat.

If we strive for peace, we must acknowledge that we live in a culture of despair, but then refuse to fall into its trap. We must hold firm to our faith in God, walk forward on the way of peace, and pursue the nonviolent transformation of ourselves and our world with great hope and determination. If we go forward in faith and do hopeful things, we will experience moments of transforming hope when we will glimpse the full possibilities of peace.

The trick is to stay hopeful, even though you've considered all the facts.

At the height of the civil rights struggle, the nuclear arms race, and the Vietnam War, Thomas Merton wrote to his friends urging them to remain hopeful. Hope for Merton was at the heart of life itself, at the core of Christian spirituality, at the center of the resurrection. "Do not depend on the hope of results," Merton wrote to Jim Forest at the Fellowship of Reconciliation in the mid-1960s. "The real hope is not in something we think we can do, but in God who is making something good out of it in some way we cannot see. If we can do God's will, we will be helping in this process. But we will not necessarily know all about it beforehand."[16]

"The quality of [our] nonviolence is decided largely by the purity of the Christian hope behind it," Merton concluded in an FOR pamphlet. "If Christians hope that God will grant peace to the world, it is because they also trust that human beings, God's creatures, are not basically evil: that there is in humanity a potentiality for peace and order which can be realized provided the right conditions are there. Christians will do their part in creating these conditions by preferring love and trust to hate and suspiciousness. The hope of the Christian must be, like the hope of a child, pure and full of trust."[17]

Merton could be hopeful because he placed his faith in God. His daily contemplative prayer before God gave him strength to proclaim words of hope in the face of the world's despair. He looked soberly at the world, yet refused to turn away in despair, and saw beyond our limitations to the promise of God's peace. He embraced the nonviolent struggle for peace and justice with the belief that God had created the world to be a haven of peace. By plunging the depths of faith and nonviolence, Merton staked his life on the hope of the risen Christ, the Gospel, and the essence of humanity itself. He encouraged us then to place our hope not in the results of our actions but in God who can use our actions to bring about change one day at a time, one step at a time, one person at a time. Because of his hope, Merton tasted the joy of life and resurrection.

In every historic struggle for peace and justice, people of peace and hope have kept their eyes on the promised land, the vision of God's reign of peace. This steadfast hope has made all the difference. From the abolitionists to the suffragists, from civil rights workers to antiwar activists, people have stood for peace and justice against enormous odds in the abiding hope that God's realm is drawing closer, that humanity can realize it, and that we can all live in peace.

It is because so many have remained hopeful and kept walking the way of peace that the world has witnessed so many powerful, revolutionary, beautiful changes in recent decades.

Nelson Mandela, Desmond Tutu, and the people of South Africa stood for decades against apartheid and refused to give up hope, even though few expected ever to see the end of apartheid. When Mandela emerged from prison after twenty-eight years and apartheid was dismantled, they kept looking forward, beyond hatred and revenge, toward the possibility of a new society based on racial and political reconciliation. This amazing accomplishment was due to the hope and commitment of the struggling people and their visionary leaders.

In 1989, nonviolent struggles in Poland, East Germany, Czechoslovakia, Bulgaria, and Hungary culminated in the fall of the Berlin Wall, an event few ever dreamed possible. At the same time, nonviolent independence movements within the Soviet Union led to the creation of Latvia, Lithuania, Estonia, Georgia, Armenia, Moldavia, and the Ukraine. During the 1980s and 1990s, we saw masses of people nonviolently bring down corrupt dictators in Haiti, the Philippines, and Indonesia. In East Timor, we witnessed a bold election for independence, after twenty-three years of brutal occupation. In Northern Ireland, Catholics and Protestants have declared a cease-fire and started to disarm after decades of "The Troubles" in the hope of forging a new peaceful coexistence.

Through the tireless work of Sister Helen Prejean and other dedicated activists, we see the emergence of a moratorium movement that heralds the abolition of the death penalty. Each day, more and more people are learning about the scores of innocent people who were nearly executed for crimes they never committed. More and more city councils, state legislatures, and governors are declaring a moratorium on executions. In Europe, the anti–death penalty movement is so strong that rallies against U.S. executions fill entire stadiums. In Rome, whenever a stay of execution or a statewide moratorium is declared in the U.S., the Coliseum is lit up all night.

Meanwhile, since 1980, over sixty "Plowshares" anti-nuclear actions have occurred. Ordinary Americans continue to walk on to military bases and enact Isaiah's vision of disarmament in the bold hope that one day, "nation will not lift up sword against nation, neither shall they study war anymore."

On November 10, 1998, I stood alone in the public gallery at the United Nations and listened as the U.N. General Assembly discussed the meaning and potential of nonviolence for the world. They had been prompted by the first-ever appeal of all the living Nobel Peace Laureates for a commitment to educate children around the world in the ways of peace. At the end of the day, the General Assembly unanimously declared the years 2001 to 2010, "A Decade for a Culture of Peace and Nonviolence for the Children of the World."

In an effort to start this new decade and new millennium in the spirit of active peacemaking, I helped organize the "People's Campaign for Nonviolence," a forty-day presence of prayer and action for peace and justice in Washington, D.C. Every day from July 1 to August 9, 2000, grassroots peace and justice groups brought several hundred people to pray, hold vigils, speak out and act for disarmament and justice at either the White House, Pentagon, or U.S. Capitol. Over 5,000 people of faith and conscience joined this summer-long witness for peace. Some groups organized events calling for the abolition of nuclear weapons and the death penalty; others proposed a mandatory living wage and amnesty for immigrants. In one day, over a hundred Jews held vigils, fasted, prayed, and lobbied for peace. The next day, over one hundred Muslims did the same. On the last day, August 9, 2000, the fifty-fifth anniversary of the U.S. atomic bombing of Nagasaki, many people gathered on the riverside lawn of the Pentagon for an inspiring interfaith prayer service for peace, led by Jews, Muslims, Hindus, Buddhists, and Christians. The whole summer of active nonviolence filled us with hope.

There are signs of hope all around us. And this hope is contagious. As we witness the daring deeds of peacemakers around the world, we too catch the spirit of hope and find the strength to take another step forward on the path to peace.

With God's help and the help of friends and community, we are able to see the many good things happening all around us. This new hope empowers us to commit ourselves anew to nonviolence, since now we know that whenever it has been tried, it has worked, and even more, that whenever we have tried it, we have experienced its transforming power in our own lives.

If we keep our eyes open for signs of hope, and stay centered in daily prayer before God, we will find ourselves taking one step after another on our life journey to peace, and before we know it, we will have lived a life of peace.

Over time, we will come to know that even if we are criticized, persecuted, arrested, imprisoned, and killed, like Jesus and Gandhi, resurrection is ours. Death will not have the last word. We know this for a fact. God has promised to lead us into the fullness of peace. And God will not let us down.

We are on a great journey. No matter how bumpy the road, we are already blessed. God's peace is ours for the asking. Indeed, it has already been given us.

There is no reason to despair.

The life of peace is as simple as our next breath.

We can take that next step on the road to peace.

From now on, we are filled with hope.

Conclusion

The life of peace is both an inner journey toward a disarmed heart and a public journey toward a disarmed
world. This difficult but beautiful journey gives infinite meaning and fulfillment to life itself because our lives become a gift
for the whole human race. With peace as the beginning, middle, and end of life, life makes sense.

Once we realize that our God is a God of peace, that we
are created to dwell in God's own peace here and now, that we
can know deep peace within our own hearts, and that we can
contribute to the peace of the world, then we will turn around
and start that journey of peace and stay with it for the rest of
our lives.

From now on, we will be filled with peace, hope, and love.

We will struggle with our inner violence and seek inner
serenity through prayer and meditation, and at the same time,

we will struggle with the world's violence and act publicly for a world of peace and justice.

We will pursue nonviolence in every facet of our lives—in our hearts, among our friends and families, in our workplace and communities, in our nation and internationally.

We will strive to end the wars in our own hearts and in the world itself through persistent reconciliation, healing love, and steadfast nonviolence.

The life of peace is a difficult balancing act between the inner work and the public work, a high-wire trapeze walk that requires calm, patient, step-by-step mindfulness toward our goal. But the journey is thrilling and the arrival at the end of the line brings joy and good cheer to everyone, on earth and in heaven.

Whether we serve the poor in a spirit of peace like Dorothy Day and Mother Teresa, or resist systemic injustice like Nelson Mandela and Martin Luther King, Jr., or teach the wisdom of nonviolence like Mahatma Gandhi and Thomas Merton, we, too, can undertake this beautiful life of peace. We need not change the whole world like these great heroes, only join the journey. That is all that the God of peace asks.

If we try, and keep trying, and stay faithful to the journey unto our last breath, we will find great joy and a peace not of this world, knowing that we serve not only the human family but the God of peace.

Nothing could be more beautiful than living peace.

Notes

1. John Dear, editor, *The Road to Peace: Writings on Peace by Henri Nouwen*. Maryknoll: Orbis Books, 1997, p. 41.
2. Thomas Merton, editor, *Gandhi on Nonviolence*. New York: New Directions, 1964, p. 6.
3. Merton, p. 24; and, Eknath Easwaran, *Gandhi the Man*. Tomales, Calif.: Nilgiri Press, 1997, p. 116.
4. Thomas Merton, *The Sign of Jonas*. New York: Image Books, 1956, pp. 261–62.
5. William Shannon, editor, *The Hidden Ground of Love: The Letters of Thomas Merton, Vol. I*. New York: Farrar, Straus and Giroux, 1985, p. 158.
6. Thomas Merton, *Thoughts in Solitude*. New York: Image Books, 1956, p. 90.
7. Thomas O'Donnell, editor, *A Thomas Merton Reader*. New York: Image Books, 1974, p. 459.
8. Merton, *Thoughts in Solitude*, p. 72.
9. Henri Nouwen, "Letting Go of All Things: Prayer as Action," in Jim Wallis, editor, *Waging Peace*. New York: Harper and Row, 1982, pp. 200–3.
10. Henry Mayer, *All On Fire: William Lloyd Garrison and the Abolition of Slavery*. New York: St. Martin's Press, 1998, p. 112.
11. For a complete account of the Smithsonian *Enola Gay* episode

225

and the history of Hiroshima, see Kai Bird and Lawrence Lif-schultz, editors, *Hiroshima's Shadow: Writings on the Denial of History and the Smithsonian Controversy*. Stony Creek, Conn.: Pamphleteer's Press, 1998.

12. Coretta Scott King, editor, *The Words of Martin Luther King, Jr.* New York: Newmarket Press, 1983, p. 25.

13. Gordon Wilson, *Marie*. London: Marshall Pickering, 1990, pp. 46–47.

14. Wilson, pp. 91–92.

15. King, p. 23.

16. William Shannon, *The Hidden Ground of Love: The Letters of Thomas Merton on Religious Experience and Social Concerns*. New York: Farrar, Straus and Giroux, 1985, p. 297.

17. Thomas Merton, *The Nonviolent Alternative*. New York: Farrar, Straus and Giroux, 1980, pp. 215–16.

About the Author

© Sally Savage Photography

JOHN DEAR is a priest, retreat leader, author, and peace activist. He has served as the executive director of the Fellowship of Reconciliation, an interfaith peace organization, and as a Red Cross coordinator of chaplains at the Family Assistance Center in New York City, after the September 11, 2001, attacks. He has traveled the world's war zones on missions of peace, been imprisoned repeatedly for civil disobedience against war, and been featured in the *New York Times*, the *Washington Post, USA Today,* and the *National Catholic Reporter,* and on NPR's *All Things Considered.* He lives in northeastern New Mexico.